how to build
a sauna

Picture courtesy of Metos Sauna, Inc., Bellevue, Washington.

how to build a sauna

Carlton Hollander

DRAKE PUBLISHERS INC.
NEW YORK · LONDON

Published in 1978 by
Drake Publishers, Inc.
801 Second Avenue
New York, N.Y. 10017

How to Build a Sauna

LC: 77-90521

ISBN: 0-8473-1673-4

Design: Harold Franklin

Printed in the United States of America

contents

To Bridget

with love

and gratitude

how to build
a sauna

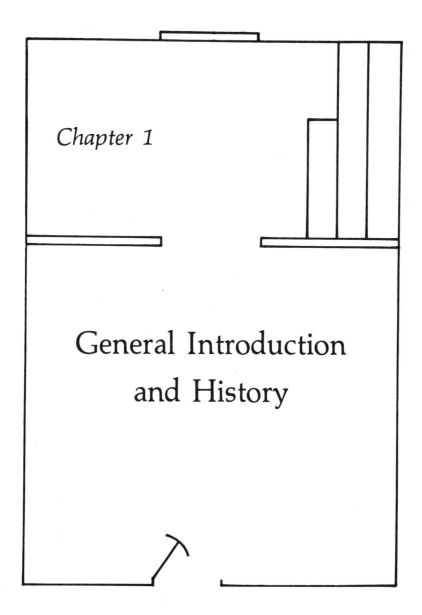

Chapter 1

General Introduction
and History

THE BASIC PURPOSE of a sauna is to cleanse the body through perspiration. This means opening the pores of the skin and flushing out the impurities in the body through the process of sweating. It is basically as simple as that, and any structure or environment that has the ability to achieve that end will suffice as a sauna. There are, however, many subtleties and nuances of a sauna that tend to make it more effective, longer lasting and more enjoyable. This book will serve as a guide to those persons who would like to build their own saunas, and a guide to the fine points which make a sauna efficacious as well as enjoyable.

The sauna of Finland is a tradition which some researchers date back over two thousand years. Many other cultures throughout the history of mankind have had similar traditions—the sweat huts of the Indians, for example—but because the culture has died out, the traditions have been lost to posterity. The Turkish bath, however, is one ancient cleansing tradition which has survived.

Equate a sauna to a Turkish bath in the presence of a Finn, however, and all you will receive is a condescending smile reserved for the ignorant. Both styles adhere to the process of cleansing through perspiration; the difference lies in the kind of heat used. The Turkish bath involves a very humid or damp heat; the Finnish sauna a dry heat. There is a difference, and advocates of both systems abound throughout the world. However, the American people seem drawn to the dry heat style of the Finns.

The traditional Finnish sauna is a very simple affair, indeed. Basically, it is a one-room hut built of hand crafted logs with a large stove in the center of the room. A fire is kept burning in the stove, and rocks (or *konnos*, as they are called) are heated on the top of the stove. The rocks become red hot, and can heat up the room to an ideal temperature of 190 to 200 degrees Fahrenheit. The bathers sit and relax in the nude on benches opposite the stove, taking in the heat for an hour or longer. During this period, the bathers normally use birch whisks as a form of stroking massage to remove perspiration from the body. It is customary and considered good manners in Finland for each person to offer to scrub the back of the other bather with the whisks. The whisks should be kept moist, thus decreasing the possible stinging sensation which would result from dry branches. Water is ladeled onto the hot rocks, creating steam which is instantly absorbed by the wood walls. Traditionally, the sauna ends with a shower and then a plunge into a cold lake or water tank. This is followed by a cooling off period in a relaxation room where the body's temperature is allowed to return to normal.

This pattern of taking a sauna alters very little throughout the world. It is simple, and according to the Finns and other exponents, extremely healthful. Aside from leaving the bather with a beautiful afterglow and mellow feeling, the Finns attribute their endurance and longevity to the tradition of sauna. They also believe in the sauna's beneficial effects on the nervous system and the mind.

The Finns, however, do not overindulge themselves in the sauna. Their traditional once a week sauna usually occurs on Saturdays for various practical reasons. Sleep is common to many sauna bathers, and a general period of cooling down, even for a few hours, is the rule. Taking a sauna cannot be a rushed process. It must be done with a sense of luxury, of taking the hours necessary to do it right. Anything less would be something of a desecration.

The evolution of the heat bath has taken three main directions. The Roman bath was primarily a dry heat bath, with very little water thrown on the rocks. Dry heat, once again, is quite popular for the simple reason that dry heat is easier to breathe than damp heat.

From the Roman bath came the Turkish bath as we know it today; plenty of humidity achieved by a constant application of water onto heated stones. The opponents of the Turkish bath claim that it is more difficult to perspire in this environment than in the dry heat baths. They will often cite respiratory difficulties arising as a result of the Turkish bath. The Turkish bath today is also known as the Russian bath, but actually the Russian bath uses much more variation in heat and moisture.

The third type of heat bath is the Japanese bath. Basically, the Japanese use two pools, one with very hot water and one with very cool water. The bather alternates between the two pools, getting scrubbed and soaped in between. Many public bathhouses in Japan still use this system, and in America, a similar bath system is becoming quite popular with those who live in luxury apartment houses and those who have backyard swimming pools. The jacuzzi, with water temperatures up to the 100 degree mark, followed by a dip in a crystal clear and very cold swimming pool, has a delightful effect upon the body.

To the purists of the perspiration bath, however, the Finnish bath is the ideal compromise—control of the humidity giving it the edge over the purely dry heat of the Roman baths or the moist heat of the Turkish bath.

There is a wealth of legend and tradition surrounding the sauna and its development through the ages. Like other peoples, the Finns believed that fire was sacred and came from the heavens. The sauna itself became a place of worship, and often sacred ceremonies took place within the confines of the stoveroom. The impurities washed through the pores of the skin were equated with devils and demons being cleansed from the body. And the steam which rose from the stones was given a special name, *loyly*, which came to mean something akin to a spiritual rising.

Surrounding these semi-religious beliefs arose a very strict and moralistic tradition. The sauna, being a sacred place, was to be viewed with the same awe as a church or other place of worship. As opposed to Roman times, when the nudity of the public bath provoked all kinds of hedonistic delights, the Finnish sauna became a very reverent undertaking. Sex was definitely out, as were voyeurism, harsh talk and obscene langauge.

In Finland today, a country with a population of about five million people, there are, at last estimate, over 700,000 saunas. The reverential attitude still exists, and the people take their bathing ritual with as much deference to tradition as possible. Many of the saunas in Finland are homemade, rustic log cabins sitting on the side of lakes of ponds. More modern saunas, however, are being built every day in the cities and suburbs. The public sauna has become quite popular, and for a fee, is available to anyone desiring the benefits of the bath.

These days the Finnish sauna is gaining popularity throughout the world, especially in the United States. There are now a few companies who manufacture saunas for the home, either in the backyard or as an attachment to an already existing structure. There are companies which furnish stoves, and even companies which supply the rocks, or *konnos*. Most gymnasiums in the United States advertise a sauna as part of their physical fitness programs, and many modern apartment complexes have saunas which are available to their tenants. Obviously, a great number of people find the sauna healthful, enjoyable and fun. But to get the most out of your sauna, it is helpful to understand the rituals behind the Finnish heat bath.

To prepare a sauna properly for use, it is important to decide first what kind of heat you desire. Moist heat, such as that found in a Turkish bath, is not as effective in stimulating perspiration as is dry heat. One of the reasons is that the moisture of the heat is often mistaken for body perspiration, and the bather is quick to jump to the conclusion tht he has cleansed himself enough. The dry heat, however, dries the skin upon entering the sauna, and it takes longer for the perspiration to really begin flowing. Thus, by the time sweat does appear on the skin, the bather is truly opening his pores and receiving the greatest benefit of the sauna.

It is essential for a successful sauna to heat the stoveroom properly. To do this, the room must be constructed as tightly and securely as possible. Heat loss will result from poor construction and heating the sauna to a proper degree will be very difficult.

But more than a well constructed stoveroom, the truly vital element of the sauna is the heated stones. The stove which you use in your sauna has one function and one function only—to heat the stones. The stove itself does nothing to radiate heat throughout the room. Its function is simple and pure. The stones themselves absorb the heat from the stove and radiate that heat throughout the sauna. And the heat which comes from the *konnos* is normally very constant, keeping the temperature of the stoveroom at a regulated level.

In ensuing chapters of this book, we will discuss in

detail the kinds of wood best used in a sauna stove. It must be hard wood, which burns hot and slow. It is advisable to light the stove and begin the heating process long before you plan to use the sauna. By doing so, you will dry out any moisture which is in the room and reach the optimum temperature.

Once the stoveroom is heated to a suitable temperature (between 190 and 200 degrees) then you are ready for the sauna. As the host of a sauna gathering, you should keep in mind that newcomers to the sauna will probably experience some shock at the heat to which they are exposed upon entering the stoveroom. Explain this to your guests so they will be prepared. Also, make sure that no one in your party suffers from heart or respiratory diseases; their systems cannot handle such intense heat.

The customary sauna involves a number of steps. First, the guests are led to a dressing room where they may shed their clothing. It is a nice touch to have towels handy for everyone—for reasons of modesty as well as for comfort once they are inside the stoveroom. Nudity is a traditional part of the sauna; bathing suits or other cover-ups are incongruous and totally uncomfortable in the heat of a sauna.

Experienced persons will probably stay inside the stoveroom for up to an hour, while novices might leave very promptly after only a few minutes. The extreme heat of a sauna takes some getting used to, and for the newcomer it is a good idea to take it slowly, one short session at a time.

The next step in the sauna process is either a quick, cold shower, or a plunge into icy water. This is probably the most exhilarating moment of the sauna. The skin pores have been opened, releasing impurities and causing a great amount of perspiration. Upon hitting the cold water, the pores quickly close as the nervous system reacts to the extreme variation in temperature. The feeling is an incredible one, and must be experienced to be believed.

After the cold water immersion, sauna takers retire to the relaxation room. This area is designed for rest, relaxation and social enjoyment after guests have soothed themselves within your sauna and feel naturally mellow and good. A little hot coffee, some light food or even some cool beer can be offered. In many traditional saunas, board games and card games are popular in the relaxation rooms. Loud music and harsh lighting are definitely out. Comfortable seating and tasteful decor will add to the post-sauna sense of well-being.

The effects of the sauna are numerous and varied. Proponents of the dry heat bath mention a feeling of psychological peace and contentment as well as physical rejuvenation. Many people claim that the sauna relieves the symptoms of minor illnesses such as colds, revives the muscles after tough physical exertion, and clears the complexion.

Basically, what happens to the body during a sauna is quite simple—the metabolism and pulse rates increase, the blood vessels become much more flexible, and the extremities benefit from increased circulation. Physical fitness fans will recognize that some of these changes can also be achieved through strenuous physical exercise. This is not to say, however, that a sauna will put you in excellent physical condition without your having to move a muscle. What it will do is bring about the same basic metabolic results as physical exercise.

In line with this is the assumption by many people that the sauna has the potential for causing weight loss. This is true to an extent. When you sweat, you do lose weight in the form of water released from body tissues. However, the weight loss is only temporary. That fluid which has been lost will be replaced naturally and you will regain those lost pounds. It should be stressed that the only sensible weight loss program is to cut calorie intake and increase physical exercise. Undoubtedly, the sauna will help at that point by firming muscle tone and increasing endurance.

Sex and the sauna is a subject which pops up often among Americans. After all, to effectively take a sauna the bather must be nude, and the thought of inviting friends, male and female alike, to strip down and enjoy your hospitality may seem somewhat suggestive to citizens of a country which legally forbids public nudity. Perhaps you will be stimulated by the sight of your partner's or friends' nudity—at first. But once inside the sauna itself, sex will be about the last thing on your mind, what with the wooden benches and a temperature of up to 200 degrees Fahrenheit.

The sauna experience itself, however, will leave you feeling very much alive. Your senses will be sharpened, and your tactile sensitivity heightened. In the vernacular of today's world, you could define the state as being "turned on." But by then the sauna will be over and what you do is your own affair.

Another aspect of the sauna which should be considered is the state of mind you are under prior to taking one. Many people attest to the healing powers of the sauna concerning mental depression and anxiety. They say that after leaving the sauna, the mind is in a relaxed, lucid state, free of the worries of the everyday world. Also, when the body feels soothed and energized, the mind and emotions often follow suit.

There are a lot of people, on the other hand, who create strange mental states through the ingestion of alcohol or drugs prior to taking a sauna. Alcohol is definitely not recommended prior to a sauna, since it works as a depressant, with a quick flash of energy leading into a state where the blood is moving slowly and the nerve endings are literally shutting down. The alcohol tends to detract from the total benefit of the sauna experience. Also, it is highly dangerous to stumble around the interior of a stoveroom. The stove and the rocks are awfully hot and one misstep could lead to a serious accident.

Incidentally, many people claim that there is nothing finer than a sauna for curing the dismal effects of a hangover. To a degree, this makes sense. The basic remedies for hangover cure, coffee and other stimulants, are recommended because they tend to energize the system and bring needed oxygen to the brain where the throbbing results of a lack of oxygen are in evidence. The sauna does stimulate the system, and therefore may act very positively in alleviating the symptoms of a hangover. Also, with drinking alcohol, one tends to accumulate an excess of body fluids. The sauna will wash those devil juices right out of your system through the miracle of sweating. Medically, however, there is still no known cure for the hangover.

A little alcohol, although not recommended prior to the sauna, is used by many people while cooling off in the relaxation room. In this state, where your body has just gone through a series of extreme changes, the alcohol should be as light as possible, such as cold beer or iced wine. Your body has lost much fluid, and is eager to replace it. Non-alcoholic beverages such as soda or juices are also refreshing at this stage of the sauna. So is a little light food.

Before taking a sauna, there are a few things you should be aware of that could result in dangerous conditions for either you or your guests. The purpose of the sauna, remember, is to put your body through some intensive changes. It is widely held that older people should not take a sauna. The strain on the cardiovascular system, it is held, is too great for elderly people to endure. Also, people with heart ailments or respiratory diseases should avoid the sauna. The best guideline to use is one of common sense. If you do suffer from a chronic ailment, check with your physician before taking a sauna.

The sauna for the newcomer can be a tremendous experience, but it can also be something of a nightmare. It is not uncommon for the initiate, when subjected to the intensive heat of the sauna, to experience dizziness, problems with breathing and a general feeling of ill health. If these symptoms arise, it is highly advisable to leave the sauna immediately. The individual may have eaten prior to entering, which is not advisable, or may be suffering from some as yet undisclosed flu or cold. The best way to treat the newcomer to the sauna is to start gradually. A temperature of around 150 degrees Fahrenheight is a good place to begin. Once accustomed to this heat level, raise the temperature in graduations of ten degrees until you have reached somewhere in the 190 to 200 degree neighborhood. In general, once the perspiration has begun to flow, you are at a good temperature. Extremely high temperatures are unsafe.

It is also a good idea to avoid drugs while taking a sauna. Tranquilizers, stimulants and other kinds of prescribed drugs do alter the body's metabolism, and may effect negatively your response to the heat of the sauna. Once again, common sense is an excellent tool.

It is best to regard the sauna within the traditions established by the Finnish people. They have used the sauna for centuries, and the rituals and habits which have developed usually exist for an excellent reason. Take your time; do not rush the event. Do not eat for at least one hour before taking a sauna. Go about your dry heat bath with serenity and dignity. Make your guests fell welcomed; watch for any signs of physical discomfort; avoid overdoing it. Generally, use the sauna with respect. You are there to have a good time and to bring health to your body and mind.

The Finns respect the sauna to such a degree that their ministers of government often conduct business in and around the sauna. The Finns believe that a man, upon leaving a fulfilling sauna, will be clear of mind and untroubled. They feel that by conducting business with men who have achieved this state, they will be able to deal sensibly and rationally with the matters at hand. They are not saying that all the world's problems would be solved if every-one just took a sauna prior to the great summit meetings of this nuclear age—but you do get the feeling that they believe it certainly couldn't hurt. And, after building your own sauna and enjoying its benefits, you just might feel the same way.

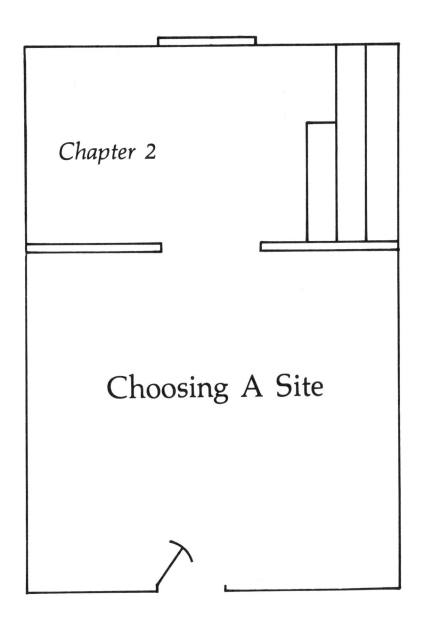

Chapter 2

Choosing A Site

THERE IS NO WAY in the world you would begin construction of a house on just any parcel of land. You would weigh, survey, and consider the advantages of each and every location available to you. The same thoroughness should be followed when choosing the location for your sauna. Where that sauna will be located will have as much bearing on its success as the quality of construction and the design itself.

If you are fortunate enough to live in the country, with access to a lake, pond or stream on your property, then the choice of where to put your sauna should be obvious. A fresh water plunge after the time spent in the stoveroom is the highest recommended form of sauna. It's virtually unbeatable. So, putting your sauna within easy access of a fresh water source should be your highest priority.

Once a site has been chosen next to a lake, pond or stream, the next consideration should revolve around the kind of land you are going to build on. If there is much sand on the site, you might consider raising the sauna on stilts, avoiding the problem of having your floor base shift with the constantly moving sand. If the ground is solid, then you would proceed with the normal base construction. Also, if there is no flat land around your water source, you need not be discouraged. Many saunas in Finland are built into the sides of hills, using the terrific insulation properties of mother earth for the three inlaid walls. You might contemplate this construction even if there is flat land available—especially if you are considering a tennis court or volleyball court on that land in the future. No need to use the level ground when a hill will do just as well.

Before taking your chain saw into the countryside behind your home and whacking down everything in sight, spend a few hours in serene contemplation of the area itself. Are there trees that would provide beauty and serenity around your sauna? Is there a more natural site a few feet away which would not involve the cutting of trees and foliage? In other words, try and situate the sauna building in the most natural and beautiful place possible.

Now, once you have that improbably beautiful site chosen, you can rough out your ground foundation (more in detail about this procedure later). Using the old string and stake technique, map out approximately where the building will go. In doing this, make sure you consider the placement of your doorways and windows.

It is important to be aware of the natural surroundings, from the foliage which could provide privacy for your sundeck, to the path of the sun year round. By charting the path of the sun, for instance, either with the casual eye or through a technically exact system used by the Weather Service, you will be insuring that your sundeck gets the most exposure possible throughout the year. Plus, you will be able to offer your sauna visitors spectacular sunsets and the beauty of moonlit nights. By thinking ahead about these matters and using mother nature's continuing show of beauty, you will be insuring a mellow, natural environment for your sauna.

Privacy is another important aspect of location which should be considered before choosing a spot. Saunas are taken in the nude, and the last thing you want is a neighborhood spectacle of naked friends romping in and out of your building to the tank or lake. This could cause genuine embarrassment and quell the spirit of the sauna adventure. To prevent this, search your land for a spot which is secluded, or possesses enough foliage to block the view of curious onlookers. If a natural wall of privacy does not exist, you might want to erect a temporary one and begin planting ivy or some other thick vegetation to cover it.

The countryside is the ideal place for a sauna: a beautiful forest setting next to a fresh water lake, with beautiful sunsets and starry nights. But for most of us, the suburban backyard is all we have to work with. By using a little imagination and forethought, however, the average backyard can be turned into a private paradise. It is only a matter of thinking ahead and utilizing the space available to you wisely.

Depending upon how much money you plan to spend, it is possible to create a luxurious environment for your sauna, complete with trees and shrubbery and the feel of totally natural surroundings. But even without these added features, the location within the backyard will be vital to the total effect which your sauna will create.

As before, knowing the path of the sun and moon are important considerations. Exposing your sundeck to the greatest amount of sunlight will add immensely to your enjoyment. The privacy factor must also be taken into consideration.

There are many practical ways to insure privacy in the backyard—from the construction of wood slats on top of an already existing fence, to the careful planting of shrubbery. Make sure you explore all the possibilities before choosing a permanent site because a suburban backyard obviously affords a much greater risk of peering eyes than does a countryside locale.

Now that you have chosen a location for your sauna which will provide as much natural beauty as possible, you must look at the legal side. Each area of the country has various building codes which must be adhered to. Call your local department of building and safety and ask them to send you the regulations and codes which apply to your sauna. Specifically, you should be aware of clearance laws, height laws and plumbing ordinances. The department usually has counselors on hand who will help you through the tangle of local ordinances, but if they don't, someone in the contracting business can be consulted. Also consider thoroughly the codes pertaining to the construction and performance of chimneys—especially in suburban areas where the ordinances tend to be very strict.

Remember, the building codes can force you at a later date to dismantle your sauna, so make sure everything you do is permitted by local law. The building inspector can be a tiger, but he can also be a helpful friend. Use him and his office to help avoid any legal entanglements before they arise.

Another aspect to choosing a good site for your sauna should be the accessibility of the sauna building itself. If your water supply dictates the location of your sauna—say, a river or lake—then you should use that as your determining factor. However, if you are going to use a man-made source for your cold water plunges, then you have a bit more freedom of choice. Some considerations which you might think about could prove valuable in the long run. Just how far is the building from the house? Will your guests have to go from a warm house into the cold of winter to get to your sauna? If you are planning a dressing room within the building itself, then there's no need to worry. Will the sauna be close enough to your water tank to make the journey from the stoveroom to the cold water pleasant? Or, will your guests immobilize due to frostbite halfway there?

In other words, check the practical aspects of your location prior to committing yourself. Try to put your sauna in the most reasonable and accessible locale possible. Remember, the sauna is for enjoyment and not a test of endurance. Consider it a part of your house, an accessory to your everyday life, and most of the location problems will work themselves out.

Finally, there may arise some problems of location when dealing with the problem of drainage. Water spillage is inevitable in and around a sauna—either from the shower inside, or the water tank outside. Your guests will be moving around inside with wet bodies, and it will be absolutely necessary to construct a good drainage system. Your choice of location can either simplify or hinder that job.

Try to avoid putting your sauna in a gulley or ditch where water, not only from the sauna but from rains, will tend to gather. If you have high ground with a natural gravity run-off, and the other conditions are satisfactory, you might consider this as a perfect spot. But watch out. Make sure the run-off will head in the direction you desire or, if not, that the possibility of digging a run-off ditch exists. The last thing you want is stagnant water collecting beneath the floorboards of your sauna. One of the finest aspects of a good sauna is its cleanliness. Make it as easy on yourself as possible, and make sure that you have a good drainage system in mind.

The final choice of location for your sauna will affect its success in the years to come. Study the problem carefully, work with what you have, and remember that almost any engineering problem can be solved with a little forethought and caution.

Following is a review of things to consider when deciding where to place your sauna.

1. Artistic considerations:

Use the natural beauty of the environment as productively as possible. Do not waste good land when you can achieve the same effect by placing your sauna in terrain less suited for other activities. Take into account the potential for sunlight, sunsets and sunrises. And use as much artistic feeling as possible to achieve practical goals such as guaranteeing privacy.

2. Building codes:

Check with your city or county first, talk with the building inspector and find out exactly what you can or cannot do. Making sure your sauna is legal before you build is worth the time and effort. The hassles later on could prove disastrous.

3. Accessibility:

Look for convenience here, and remember that sauna is a year-round tradition. You don't want to freeze your friends out of existence.

4. Drainage:

Keep in mind the run-over from your sauna, and remember the old lowland/highland aspects of water flow. You do not want a marsh beneath the floorboards of your sauna, nor do you want water trickling down a slope into your den. More about constructing a drainage system beneath the sauna later.

In the beginning of this chapter, we discussed the ideal location—next to a lake or a river. Most of us will not have that option, and will have to work within the confines of a backyard. And although the purists might disagree, the proper selection of a site and the imaginative development of an environment can make any sauna just as beautiful and functional as one which sits on the banks of one of Finland's 100,000 lakes.

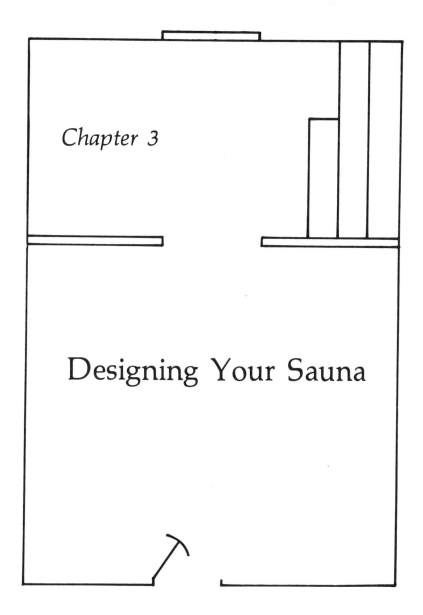

Chapter 3

Designing Your Sauna

NOW THAT YOU HAVE CHOSEN the location for your sauna, the next logical step is to create a useful, pleasing design for your building. In doing so, the actual procedures involved in taking a sauna must be considered on a step-by-step basis.

The typical sauna will involve as the first step, undressing. Naturally, you will want this particular area somewhat private, and large enough to accommodate the act in comfort. Afterwards, the visitor will go to the stoveroom, or actual sauna room, and enjoy the dry heat. Considerations begin to emerge as to how far away from the stoveroom the dressing room should be, taking into account the fact that you and your guests will be without clothing at this stage. After the time spent in the stoveroom, your guests will then head for the water tank, shower, or lake, if there is one handy. Your basic design should allow for easy access to the water supply. In the dead of winter, running from the stoveroom to a water source could prove highly unpleasant. Once the actual heat/bathing cycle is completed, you will then need a room for rest and relaxation. This room should be comfortable yet low-keyed.

Also to be considered when creating a basic design are areas for storage of wood, towels, etc. These areas should be separated from the water supply areas because it is necessary to maintain dryness at all times. Wet wood does not burn well, and damp towe deery unpleasant.

The dressing room, water source and stoveroom are absolutely necessary in a functional sauna. But the storage area and relaxation room can be optional, or at least combined with the other rooms at the discretion of the builder. A storage room combined with dressing room, for instance, will work and will not impede the effectiveness of the sauna itself. However, a dressing room and a washroom would not be advisable because of the moisture which will abound as a result of steaming bodies and the humidity created by the water and the heat. So, if you are inclined to combine certain aspects of the sauna, make sure one function will not destroy another.

Once you have decided what you want in your sauna, the next step is to begin drawing simple designs which will

Design:

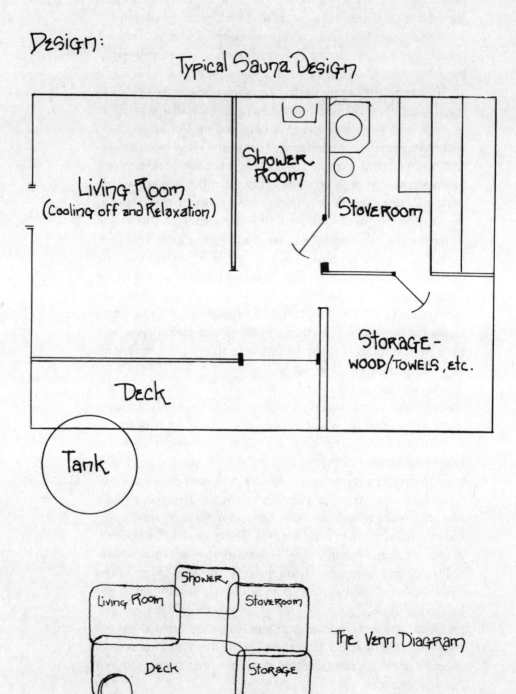

Typical Sauna Design

Living Room
(Cooling off and Relaxation)

Shower Room

Stove Room

Storage –
Wood/Towels, etc.

Deck

Tank

The Venn Diagram

Living Room
Shower
Stove Room
Deck
Storage

accommodate these features. Architects use a very ingenious, yet simple system called the Venn diagram for just such a purpose. The Venn diagram consists of overlapping circles, with each circle representing a function or a room. By using this method, you can begin to picture on paper exactly how your sauna will be constructed, and how and where each room should be laid out.

In drawing your Venn diagram, the steps of the sauna procedure, as we discussed before, should be situated according to their various functions. Remember that the stoveroom should be situated so that it is readily accessible to the shower or the tank. The relaxation, or cooling room, should be accessible to the dressing room, without the bathers having to move through a stoveroom or a washroom into that area once they have cooled off. In other words, design the sauna so that each step may be reached without having to backtrack through any of the others. Some of the simple diagrams included here will illustrate those points further.

Once the basic design has been completed, it is necessary to begin analyzing each room and its function. In this way, the separate designs for those rooms will provide the ingredients which make for a successful sauna.

The Dressing Room:

The dressing room is the first step of the sauna. You might want to forego this room entirely if the location of your stoveroom is close enough to the house so as to allow your guests to undress outside the sauna. However, if you do include a dressing room, there are certain aspects which should be considered.

First, account for the number of people who will be using your sauna at any one time. The normal recommendation is that the dressing area (if it also is to be used as a relaxation room), be about the size of the stoveroom. If the relaxation room is to be separate, then the dressing room should be about half the size of the stoveroom. In taking into account the number of people who might be occupying this room at any one time, little things such as the number of clothes pegs, a rack for shoes, shelves for watches, glasses, etc., and mirrors should be considered. Also, benches are a nice addition for people who find it difficult, as most of us do, to remove their shoes from a standing position.

Water on the floor can create an unpleasant and chilling atmosphere in the dressing room. The easiest solution, one which should be considered even if you have an excellent drainage system in your sauna, are duckboards. These slatted boards will allow the water to drain beneath the floor and prevent puddles, and in colder climates, ice, from developing.

The dressing room, then, should be designed with the number of people who will be using it at any one time in mind. By thinking of them and their comfort, you will come up with your own little touches for proper and friendly accommodation. One abstract note: the dressing room is the beginning and the end of a sauna, and by achieving a favorable environment you will ensure the total success of your sauna.

The Stoveroom:

The stoveroom is, after all, the focus of a sauna. It is the room in which the actual heat bathing will take place. Therefore, its design is vital to the success of your sauna.

The Finnish Building Information Institution has recommended specific dimensions for the size and shape of stoverooms compiled through years of research into their national pastime known as sauna. Starting with their basic figure, the Institution recommends that a stoveroom allow for 105 cubic feet per bather. This figure is not necessarily an absolute, and many people are discovering that it is, indeed, a very generous allowance of space.

But by using this basic figure, you can compute the approximate size of your stoveroom as follows. Say the number of people planned for is ten and the ceiling is a conventional height of 7 feet. You then divide the figure of

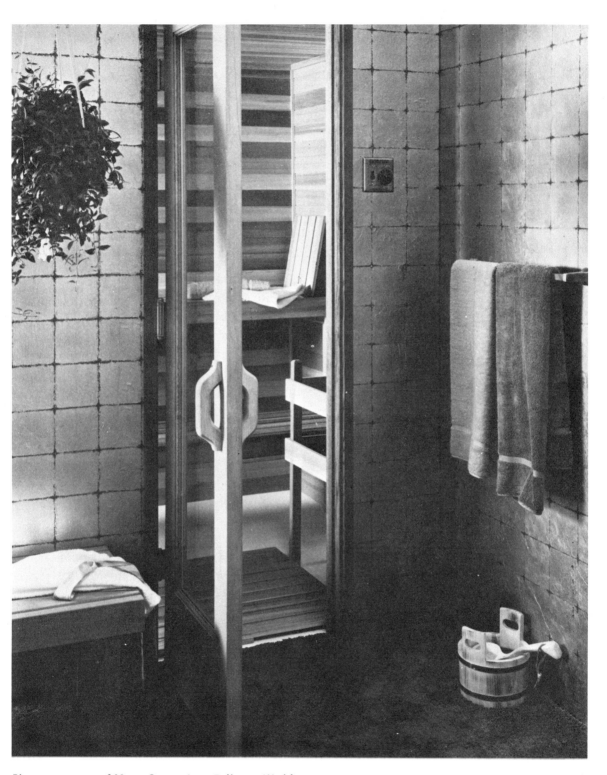

Picture courtesy of Metos Sauna, Inc., Bellevue, Washington.

1,050 cubic feet (10 x 105 cubic feet) by 7. That figure is 150 cubic feet. Now, figuring that your stoveroom will be as close to a perfect square as possible, you simply take the square root of that 150 and you have the length of your walls. In this case, a wall length of 12 feet (12 x 12 equals 144 square feet), which is close enough to the magic number of 1,050 cubic feet. So, if you want to stay within the Finnish Building recommendation, you should design your stoveroom to be 12 x 12 x 7 feet if you plan to seat ten people at a time. As we mentioned before, however, the figure of 105 cubic feet per bather is not necessarily an absolute, and many people find that they can accommodate many more people per cubic foot than is recommended by the Finnish.

An important consideration in designing the size of the stoveroom is the temperature, a larger room taking much more time to heat. A medium sized room, say, 8 x 10 x 7, if designed with the best use of seating space, will accommodate up to 12 people very comfortably, while not being a burden to heat. There is also the fact that sometimes only two or three people will be using the sauna, and to heat a huge room just for that number can be discouraging. So, a moderately sized room, but one which will accommodate friends, is the perfect compromise.

Once the size of the stoveroom has been determined, the actual shape of the room should be designed. Recommended highly is a square or rectangular room with a sloped ceiling, the angle rising from the wall which backs the stove to the far wall underneath which are the benches. The top bench itself, in a design of this type, should be a minimum of 42 inches from the ceiling, allowing the occupants of the room to move about. The sloped ceiling is logically a fine idea, and not too difficult to construct. Since heat rises, the heat from the stove itself will tend to move to the highest point in the room—that being the opposite wall where the ceiling is at its apex. Thus, the bathers sitting closest to the stove will receive the heat as it passes by them on its way to the heights. A sloping ceiling should begin at about 5½ feet and angle upwards to a height of 7 feet.

Experiments are now being made with round rooms,

trapezoidal rooms and dome shaped saunas. According to those who have had the pleasure of using these facilities, the odd shapes work very well indeed. But for the home builder, simple construction is a major consideration, and the square or rectangular room with the simple sloping ceiling seems the most practical and the most effective design.

The layout of the benches within the stoveroom is also a major point of consideration. You may wish to consider any number of schemes—from the L-shaped to the U-shaped to the straight across stepped version. The important thing to remember, however, is that you should maximize your sitting space and minimize your walking space. Bathers inside a sauna do not move about; they recline or sit during their bath. Thus, the important element is to have the benches arranged for maximum comfort and accessibility.

In designing your bench scheme, a few vital statistics on the average size of the benches themselves should be noted. In order to allow space not only for sitting, but for reclining, the width of the bench should be a foot and a half to two feet. This will allow your bathers to assume any number of positions easily and comfortably. The height of the benches should be somewhere in the neighborhood of 16 inches, creating a comfortable angle for sitting upright. Lengthwise, it's a good idea to make the benches as long as that area of your stoveroom so as to utilize as much space as possible.

The remainder of the stoveroom design should be dealt with on a very practical level. The door to the room, for instance, should, for safety reasons, always open outwards.

The stove itself must be accounted for—its position, size, and the type of stove. a wood burning stove, for instance, should have an area set aside for the logs plus a chimney for the smoke. An electric or gas stove needs only room for itself.

The ventilation factor is important, and with proper planning, can achieve a number of functions. First, a fresh air intake vent should be situated behind the stove itself, a few inches off the floor. The vent should be between 6 and 12 inches wide and should take in air directly from the outside. The other vent should be at the farthest point possible from the intake vent, ideally a few inches from the ceiling on the opposite wall. If possible, this vent should lead into the dressing room or relaxation room to supply heat. By designing your ventilation system properly, you will have achieved two important functions with one stroke—the continual circulation of fresh air in the stoveroom, and the heating of other parts of the sauna building.

Often, however, it is impossible to construct the ideal ventilation system, and with a wood burning or gas burning stove with its own ventilation system you might feel that nothing else is needed. The fresh air intake is important, though, and there are ways of easily solving the problem. The simplest method is to cut an inch or so off the bottom of your stoveroom door, allowing the air from the outer extremities of the sauna building to enter the stoveroom.

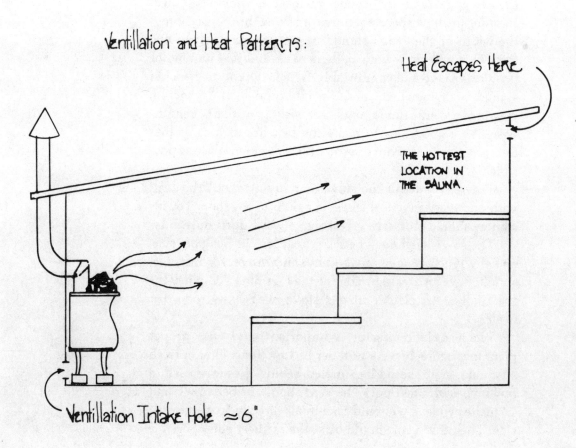

Ventillation and Heat Patterns:

Heat Escapes Here

THE HOTTEST LOCATION IN THE SAUNA.

Ventillation Intake Hole ≈ 6"

Picture courtesy of Metos Sauna, Inc., Bellevue, Washington.

In conclusion, then, when designing the stoveroom, take into consideration these basic features: the size and shape, the location of the benches, the kind of stove you will be using, the ventilation system best geared to that stove type, the door, and the maximum use of space to accommodate the bathers. Once the actual size of the room has been determined, you should then be able to design the interior accommodations by using the basic figures that we have provided.

Remember that the stoveroom itself is the major focus of your sauna, and should be designed with that in mind.

The Washroom/Tank Area

The washroom itself may serve a multitude of purposes, and then again, depending upon your situation, may not be necessary at all. According to the Finns, a washroom is a necessity if your sauna is not located close to a natural water source. It is customary in Finland to shower or cleanse oneself before entering the stoveroom. Although hygienically sensible, it is not vital to shower prior to taking a sauna. So, if a washroom is for one function and you have limited amounts of money available for the construction of your building, you may decide that the shower room is totally unnecessary.

If, however, you do not have a water source such as a tank or a tub available for immersion between bouts inside the stoveroom, your washroom will become a must. Sauna is much more than merely heating up inside the stoveroom. It involves the continual changing of heat and environment—from the stoveroom to a cool water source and back again. The shower room, complete with a device as simple as a hose and inexpensive shower head, will do in a pinch as a substitute for complete immersion. If that is the case, then the normal consideration for space and size should be made. Taking the measurements of a normal bathroom and applying them to the design of the shower room should work. In other words, make the room as comfortable as possible, and readily accessible to the stoveroom because your guests will undoubtedly make a number of trips between the two rooms.

If, on the other hand, you are going all out on your sauna and plan to build or install a tank outside your sauna, then you might consider dropping the notion of a washroom altogether.

The tank itself, for total immersion after the heat of the sauna, can be as simple or as elegant as you desire, or can afford. But in placing your water tank, you should remember once again the functions of this particular addition.

First of all, the tank should be readily accessible to the stoveroom. Your guests will be leaving the stoveroom, and temperatures up to 200 degrees Fahrenheit, and running or walking speedily to the water tank. The tank itself should be large enough for a normal sized human being to recline in. The hot tubs which are becoming so popular these days are an excellent size, and because they are built for the purpose of hot tub bathing, might be the perfect choice. They would provide two functions, and thus be well worth the price. If a redwood tub is out of the question, then you might consider a huge tub, if that is available.

The tank's size and width should, as mentioned before, be large enough for a normal sized human being. The depth should be enough to allow a person to be completely submerged. You will find that by making the tub large enough to accommodate one reclining man, you will have enough room inside for four to six people in a sitting position. This is important because the tub can, in reality, become a social gathering place outside the stoveroom of your sauna. And with careful planning, it can also serve a multitude of functions.

When designing space for your tub, a few vital facts must be considered. First, a tub large enough to accommodate four to six people will generally weigh within the area of two or more tons. Water is quite heavy, in case you haven't noticed. So, if the tub is to be raised on a platform outside the stoveroom, make sure you have taken the weight factor into consideration. If the tub is to be placed directly on the ground surface, check out the terrain around it, making sure there are no strange angles or slide potentials in the ground.

Secondly, the tub will contain lots of water, and your guests will undoubtedly be sloshing water around in great amounts as they leap in and out of the tub. The greatest preventative against your guests bringing unwanted water into the stoveroom and dressing areas is simply a raised platform of duckboard ringing the entire tub. The water will drain immediately through the slats, and it will become impossible for it to collect. The duckboards are inexpensive, easy to install, and absolutely effective. Drainage from the duckboards down is another matter and will be discussed later.

The Relaxation Area

This area need not be a room with a single purpose. Basically, the function of the relaxation area is to allow your guests to recline, cool off, and lower their body temperatures to normal. This room precedes the final step of the sauna which involves dressing and leaving. Obviously, this room should be attractive and comfortable. Luxurious accomodations are popular in rooms like these, from comfortable sofas to expensive game boards and coffee makers. If possible within your budget, simple touches such as a coffee maker and board games add a nice aura to the room. But all that is really necessary is having a place where your guests can relax in comfort.

There are a number of ways to design your relaxation area so that it serves a dual purpose with other rooms of the sauna building. It is quite possible to combine your storage area with the relaxation room, dividing the room in half— one area for storage, the other with chairs or benches. Or, if your water tank is to be outside on a screened-in deck, then by adding a few deck chairs and lounge chairs you will be able to create a very pleasant atmosphere. Of course, if you live in a climate which includes severe winters, you will be well advised to keep the relaxation area indoors.

The relaxation area, then, can be anything you want it to be. It is up to you and the amount of money you wish to spend. Remember, however, that its presence is desirable within the framework of a "total sauna."

A good, substantial design of your sauna prior to actual construction is a must. No builder worth his salt will ever begin construction without some blueprint to follow, and neither should the builder of a home sauna. Remember, however, that intricate designs and strange angles and pitches are unnecessary, and may not add to the aesthetics of your sauna. The best advice is to keep it as simple as possible, make it functional, and add touches of artistic beauty whenever possible. The true Finnish sauna is of very simple design with functionalism as its architectural theme.

If you follow the steps presented in this chapter, you should be able to come up with a sensible, practical design for your sauna that will become a reality in your backyard. If problems arise from your design, or you become stuck at certain points, check with your local lumberyard or with a building contractor.

The next step, after you have the design ready to go, is the actual construction. In the following chapters we proceed through the various steps of that construction, beginning with, of course, the foundation and the floor.

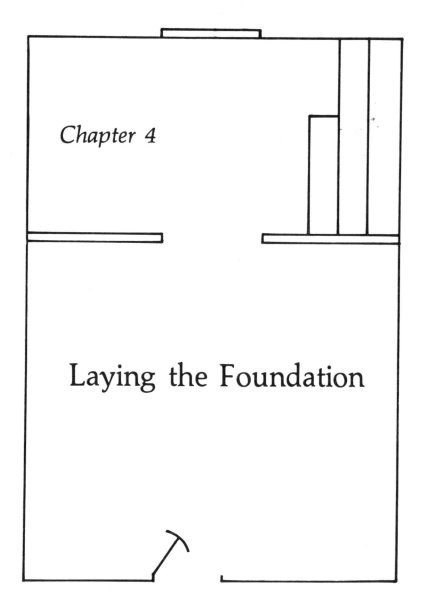

Chapter 4

Laying the Foundation

AS THE NAME IMPLIES, the foundation is the absolute core of any building. Without it, the structure cannot exist; and, if built poorly or haphazardly, the chances of the building's lasting very long are slight. The foundation is the first actual building you will do, and its construction is vital to the success of the rest of the structure. Do it well, and you are off to a running start with your sauna.

Prior to starting your foundation, it might be wise to think about the drainage system you might have to install. The water which you will need to evacuate from your stoveroom and washroom will come normally from cleaning these facilities. You will find that by hosing down the two rooms, you will be able to maintain a fine, clean environment which is important to a successful sauna. The problem is simply how to drain off that excess water.

In the next chapter, there will be tips on how to angle your floor to provide for water drainage. With a concrete slab beneath the floorboards, this is a simple solution which is accomplished by drilling a small hole into your floor at the uppermost level of your pitch. Also, if you have gravel beneath your floorboards, a simple pipe leading from the floor and down into the gravel with drainage tiles at the end will solve your problem. Remember also that the water flow need not necessarily be of its own accord; a little help from a broom can push the water to any drainage outlet you design, so there is flexibility in how you set it up. Just remember to give it some forethought prior to designing your foundation.

There are a number of ways of building a foundation. Most depend upon the terrain and soil composition of the sauna site. Poured concrete, posts and beams, and simply packed dirt are but a few ways of building a foundation. The most widely used, and probably the strongest and most efficient, is poured concrete.

The crucial task in building a foundation is to make sure that it is square and level. It is absolutely imperative later on that these qualifications be met; otherwise you will have to deal with crooked walls and problems with putting up your roof.

With a little help from Pythagoras, the task of laying out a perfect square can be simplified to its basic elements.

Consider first that a squared-off foundation consists of four right triangles at each corner of the foundation. No matter how long your walls are to be, this rule holds. So, the first chore is to lay out perfect right angles at the intersection of your lines, or walls, as they will eventually become. The best way to accomplish this is to use arcs and the basics of the Pythagorean theory.

Once you have achieved the perfect square or rectangle, the next step is to adjust the height and level off the lines which connect the actual corners of your foundation. To do this, you can construct batter boards outside the actual corners, with strings attached to them and their level horizontal boards.

Now, you must decide on the type of foundation you want. A good one is the poured concrete footing, using a trench approximately twenty inches below ground. Pouring concrete yourself may save money, but it is a difficult chore. Often, it is advisable to hire a professional and have him do the pouring. Not only will you get a top job, but also a lot of advice.

If you use a poured concrete footing, you will have to consider anchor bolts, hanging joists or nailed joists, and other headaches which could bring you more work than desired.

However, there is an alternative. In areas where cold or freezing weather does not shift the ground to such an extent as to cause structural damage, you might want to consider a simple concrete pour across a flat surface. To accomplish this, once again dig a trench along the line of your foundation, preferably about six inches in depth. Then, dig out the interior flat surface about four inches and level it. Pour an inch or two of sand on this lowered surface and level it. Next, cover the sand and trenches with polyethylene plastic, a good thickness being somewhere in the four to six mil area. Smooth this plastic down, then construct wood forms around the edges of the foundation, keeping them about two inches above ground. When the concrete is poured, this

Using Batter Boards to Square A Foundation

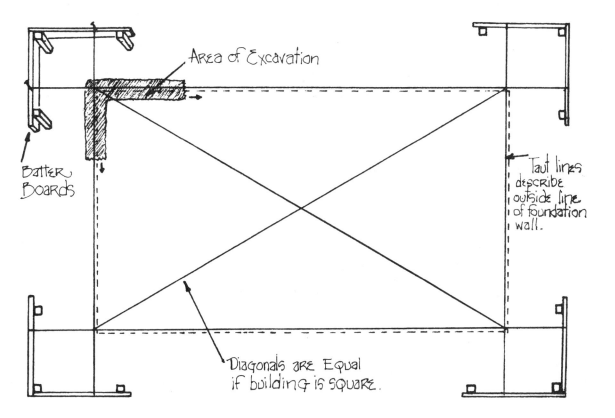

Area of Excavation

Batter Boards

Taut lines describe outside line of foundation wall.

Diagonals are Equal if building is square.

height of the form boards will raise the level of the floor some inches above the ground surface.

Now, you are ready to pour. Using a shovel and a float, work the concrete in between the reinforcing slabs around the perimeter. A good idea here is to take into account your drainage plans. You might want to smooth out the stove-room floor surface so that it pitches to a slight angle (an inch pitch is enough for proper drainage), thus preventing the problem of drainage later on. Also suggested by most builders as they pour concrete foundations is the addition of wire mesh about an inch from the bottom inside the concrete itself. Actually, any kind of steel inside the concrete helps to reinforce the structure, so try to get something inside that form before it dries.

Prior to the hardening of the concrete you should consider the attachment of a sill plate around the form itself. This is easily done with 3/8 or 1/2 inch threaded rod, ten inches long, that you will place into the concrete in a verti-

Concrete Slab Foundations

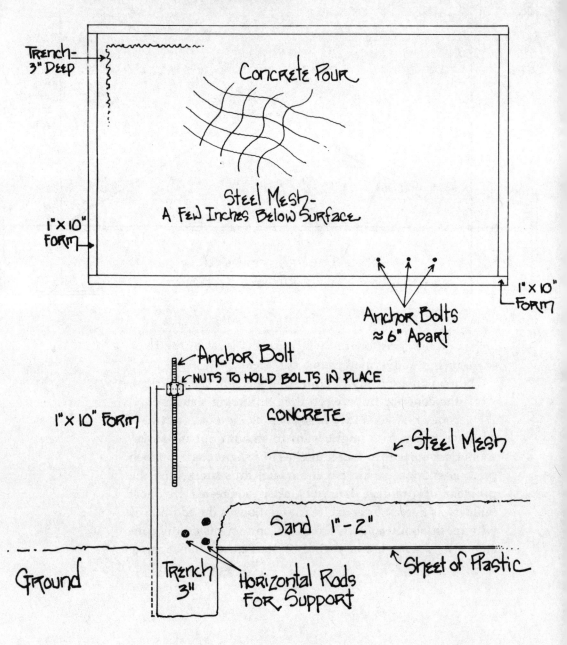

Trench— 3" Deep

Concrete Pour

Steel Mesh— A Few Inches Below Surface

1"x10" Form

Anchor Bolts ≈ 6" Apart

1"x10" Form

← Anchor Bolt
← NUTS TO HOLD BOLTS IN PLACE

1"x10" Form

CONCRETE

← Steel Mesh

Sand 1"-2"

Ground

Trench 3"

Horizontal Rods For Support

↑ Sheet of Plastic

Foundation:

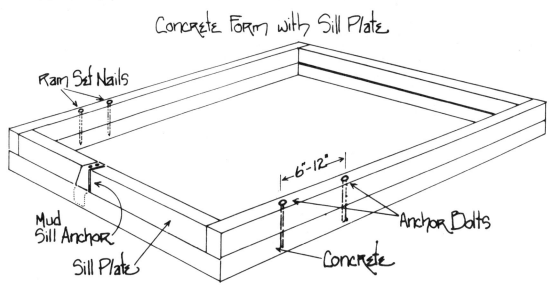

Concrete Form with Sill Plate

Ram Set Nails

Mud Sill Anchor

Sill Plate

|←6"-12"→|

Anchor Bolts

Concrete

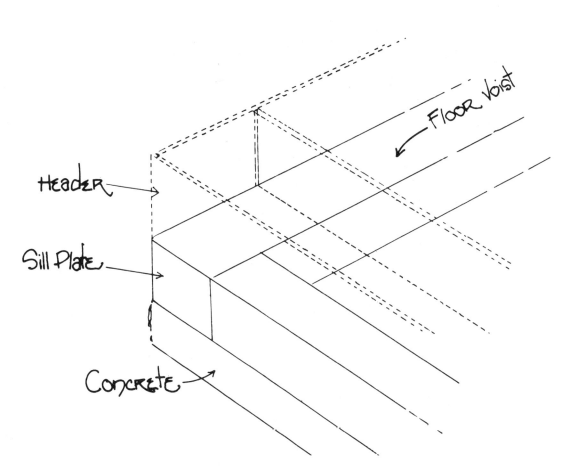

Header

Sill Plate

Concrete

Floor Joist

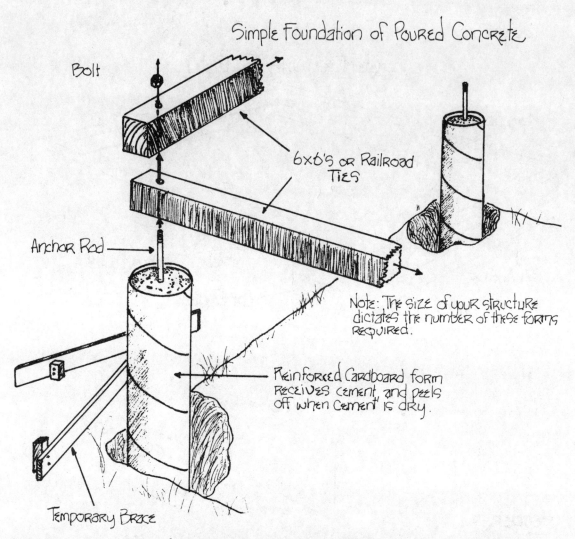

Simple Foundation of Poured Concrete

Bolt

6x6's or Railroad Ties

Anchor Rod

Note: The size of your structure dictates the number of these forms required.

Reinforced Cardboard form receives cement, and peels off when cement is dry.

Temporary Brace

cal position every four feet or so. Allow the rod to stick up about three inches above the surface (use a nut to hold it at that level).

Another method of attaching the sill plate to the concrete form is the mud sill anchor. This is simply a piece of metal which is placed into the concrete and when the concrete dries, bent across the top of the sill plate and secured there. These are available at any hardware store, and the proper sizes and fixtures for your particular foundation can be suggested by the professional dealer.

Another foundation which is quite popular and quite effective is the railroad tie foundation. Basically, it's as simple as laying down four or more railroad ties, securing them with hinges, and insulating the interior of the frame. By in-

Concrete Block Foundation Reinforced with Poured Concrete

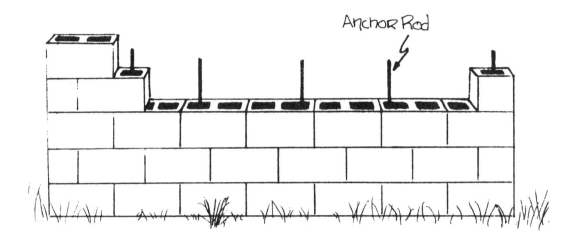

Anchor Rod

Poured Concrete

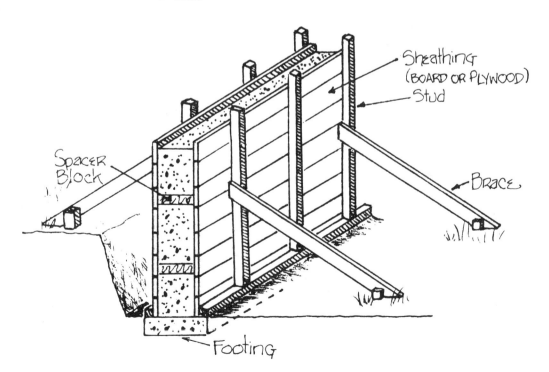

Sheathing
(BOARD OR PLYWOOD)

Stud

Spacer Block

Brace

Footing

Floor:

Girder Construction

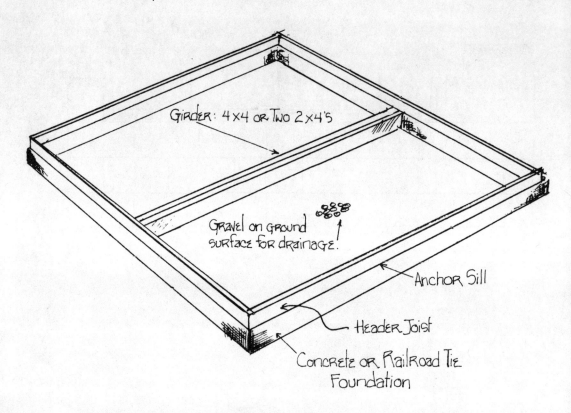

Girder: 4×4 or Two 2×4's

Gravel on ground surface for drainage.

Anchor Sill

Header Joist

Concrete or Railroad Tie Foundation

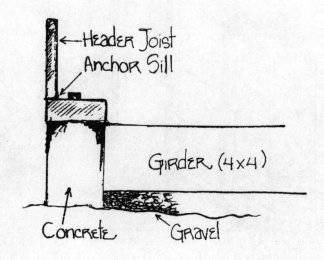

Header Joist
Anchor Sill

Girder (4×4)

Concrete   Gravel

sulation, we mean a layer of gravel on the earth, some plastic on top of that and across the ties, and the wood over that. Duckboard is a fine floor base because water will go through the slats and be absorbed by the gravel. You might want to put another layer of gravel over the plastic, creating a very nice drainage system. This also serves as a fine insulation since it lies directly beneath the duckboard.

The railroad tie foundation is a good one, but its use demands flat ground. You must first level the area where you are going to lay the ties if this foundation is to be acceptable. One other problem is securing the ties themselves. In a foundation like this, the wood frame will receive much moisture, and regular wood will rot. Railroad ties, however, are coated and will last for years. Contact your local railroad for the ties and try to get them at a salvage price.

The railroad tie foundation when completed is very simple and easy to work with. The wall studs can be nailed directly to the ties, and the basic foundation for your walls is provided.

Another foundation which does not use concrete is what is known as the hanging post foundation. This system involves a series of posts secured in the ground, either by concrete or gravel, and the frame hung and fastened around them. This foundation is very good for non-level surfaces where you can adjust the level and height of your basic frame. This foundation is easily built by digging post holes

Railroad Tie Foundation:

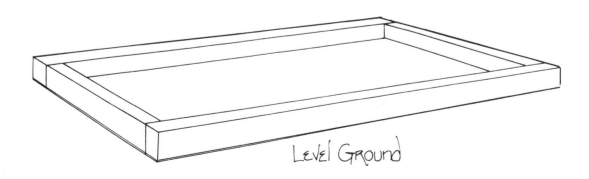

Level Ground

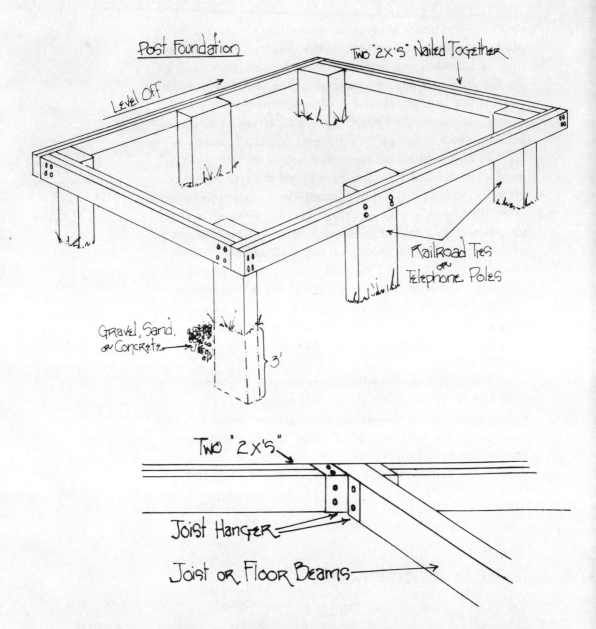

Post Foundation

Level Off

Two "2X's" Nailed Together

Railroad Ties or Telephone Poles

Gravel, Sand, or Concrete

3'

Two "2X's"

Joist Hanger

Joist or Floor Beams

at least three feet deep, putting in railroad ties or telephone poles, and securing them with enough gravel or concrete (eight to ten inches worth) to maintain their strangth. Then, simply hang your foundation walls of 2 x 6 boards around the perimeter. The most effective and strongest method of securing these frames is to nail two pieces together, thus giving you a 4 x 6-inch plank going around the perimeter of the floor. This structure will serve as your floor base and the basic foundation for your wall.

Once the square foundation is in place, you may then hang your floor boards, or joists, between the boards ringing your foundation. This can be accomplished through a number of methods, the most popular and technically most proficient being the stirrup or joist hanger. It is customary to hang the joists anywhere from 16 to 24 inches apart (this measurement is always taken from the center of one board to the center of another). Talk to your lumber man about the size of your joists—he will probably tell you that a 2 x 4 is good enough for your purposes.

Now that the joists are in place, you are ready to begin securing your floor—using plywood, planks, or even duckboards. Also, the wall base is now in place and ready for construction.

The methods for constructing your foundation are up to you and many times will be dictated by the lay of your land and the climate in which you live. The complex concrete poured foundations, with their supports and rod supports are the most difficult. The flat pour is a fairly simple method and should be accessible to anyone. The wood frame foundations, either the flat railroad tie or the hanging post type, are even easier. All are effective and should provide a foundation with the strength and durability needed to support the remainder of the building.

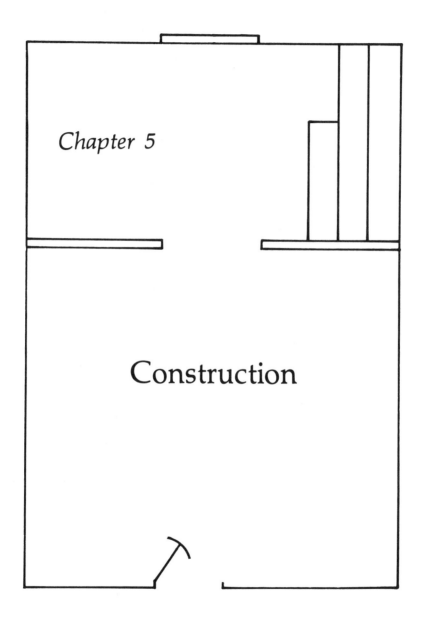

Chapter 5

Construction

THIS CHAPTER COVERS the actual building of your sauna floor, walls and roof. There is a discussion of the various methods of insulation and paneling, and directions on how to install them in and around your stoveroom. You will need to fit in a door, and possibly a window. Finally there is information on the various methods for lighting your stoveroom. If you use this chapter as a guide to actual construction, your own sauna should soon be a warm and glowing possibility.

The Floor:

The foundation is set, and the next step is to build your floor. The materials used here depend upon your tastes and finances. The most popular floor for a stoveroom is usually wood, often one-inch plywood, with duckboards to facilitate movement. Some sauna companies recommend using fiberglass and stainless steel, but the aesthetics of the traditional sauna will be lost with these modern materials. The second most popular floor is simply concrete, which we will discuss first.

A concrete floor is made by pouring a flat mat foundation. Most people who use the concrete generally wind up placing duckboards across the surface, which are removable for easy cleaning. Concrete advocates stress easy cleaning and the inherent quality of being fireproof as advantages. But fires in stoverooms are extremely rare in the first place.

A good way to circumvent the natural problem in concrete, that being its ability to gather and conduct cold, is to insulate the slab with a layer of gravel beneath. The gravel will absorb much of the cold and prevent if from emerging through the concrete itself.

But the easiest and cheapest floor to build is a wooden one. You don't have to bother with the pouring of concrete, and the materials are workable and pliable. Also, wood happens to be one of the finest natural insulators around. The purists will argue that a stoveroom floor made of anything other than wood is just not in keeping with the sauna tradition. They will also argue that for pure aesthetics, there is nothing quite like wood.

Girder, Floor Construction Using Hanging Joists

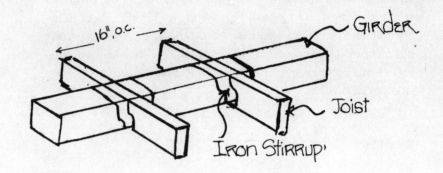

16", o.c.

Girder

Joist

Iron Stirrup

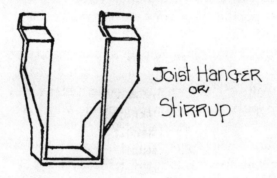

Joist Hanger
OR
Stirrup

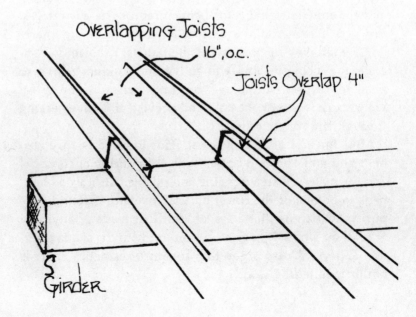

Overlapping Joists

16", o.c.

Joists Overlap 4"

Girder

If your foundation is on a raised level, you will need to consider some type of insulation beneath the floor itself and the ground below. The purpose of this insulation will be to form an air pocket beneath the floor, and keep out any winds that might blow up through the cracks in your floorboard and destroy the heat of the sauna. If, however, your floorboard will be resting on terra firma, with the gravel we mentioned before beneath, there will be no need to insulate.

Once you have hung your joists and are ready to lay down the floorboard itself, it is time to insulate. A good insulation structure involves three phases—a top layer of polyethylene cardboard stretched across the tops of the joists themselves to seal the floor; a layer of foil-covered insulation beneath that; and waxed cardboard or some other water sealant material directly beneath the foil insulation. Some builders suggest that styrofoam between the cardboard layers is fine, and cheaper to use. This is up to you. (The diagram will show how to organize your materials).

Floor Construction Using Girders

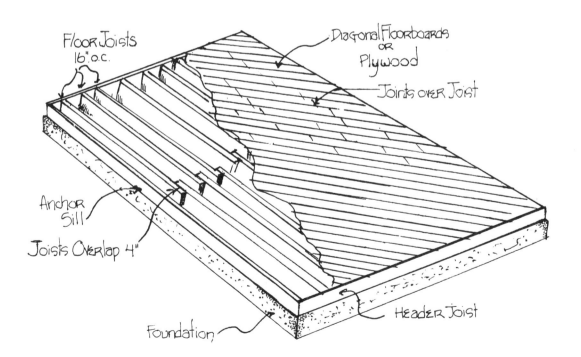

Insulation:

A. Foundations

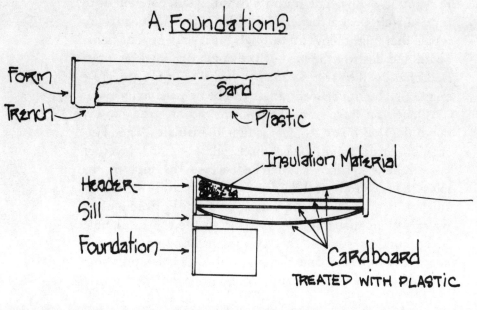

B. Walls

Once your insulation is in place, then it is merely a matter of laying down your plywood (one-inch thick) with the smooth surface up. Nail the wood to the joists and you have your floor. Some people prefer using wood planks as their floor base, claiming that the aesthetics are greater than mere plywood. Of course it is up to you. But the important thing to remember about your floor is the insulation. Without it, you might find that your sauna is unworkable, especially if you reside in areas where strong, cold winds might seep up beneath the structure. Once again, forethought is the key. Take the time to study the matter.

Once your floor and its insulation are in place, there are little touches which might add to the comfort and utility of the floor itself. We've previously discussed duckboards and their function. It is quite possible to lay a series of these boards across your plywood and provide your floor with another layer of wood. Also possible are cocomats, the kind you see on the floors of sports cars. They are very resilient, and may be taken off the floor for cleaning. Just remember that whatever you decide to lay on top of the plywood must be something of a thermal insulator. The floor inside your sauna can become very hot, so avoid plastics or other materials which may melt or become disfigured as a result of the heat.

Insulating the Walls:

Once your floors have been secured and completed, it is time to begin structuring your walls. Prior to the actual construction, it would be wise to consider the kind of insulation you wish to use when it comes time to actually panel the walls. This same consideration should be taken with the roof. The steps involved here are first, the construction and raising of the wall frames into place, and second, the construction and fastening of the roof, after which you lay in your insulation. But choosing that insulation beforehand will make things much simpler when you reach the stage of securing your paneling onto the wall and roof structure.

Insulation of your walls will provide you with two important functions. It will decrease the humidity inside the stoveroom (after all, a sauna is normally used with the driest heat possible) and it will decrease the heat loss through the walls themselves. Unless the stoveroom is built with incredible quality, you are bound to experience some kind of heat loss through the walls, and it is best to insulate to guarantee a thorough retention of your heat.

For the outside wall of your sauna, you should think in terms of a vapor barrier. This can be as simple as nailing sheets of aluminum foil one mil thick to the outer wall studs. The permeability level of this substance is practically nil, so nothing will escape. If, in purchasing your foil, you

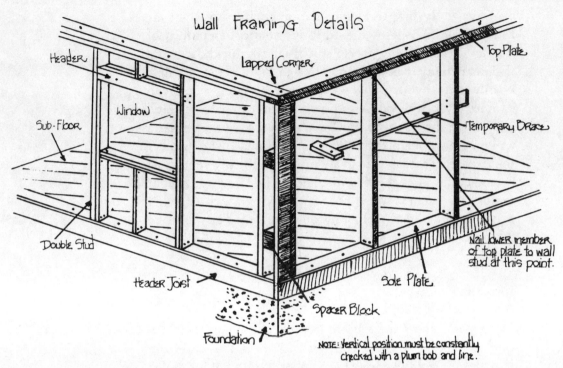

Wall Framing Details

Header · Window · Sub-Floor · Double Stud · Header Joist · Lapped Corner · Foundation · Spacer Block · Sole Plate · Top-Plate · Temporary Brace · Nail lower member of top plate to wall stud at this point.

NOTE: vertical position must be constantly checked with a plum bob and line.

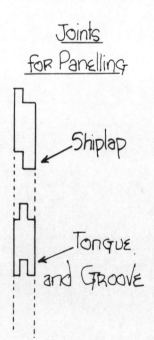

Interior Walls:

Joints for Panelling

Shiplap

Tongue and Groove

find that the aluminum paper is coated, with one side shinier than the other, turn the shinier side inside towards the interior of your stoveroom; you will then be reflecting the heat back into the sauna itself.

Once the outer wall is secured with insulation, you must deal with the inner wall, the area between the interior paneling and the outside wall. Normally, the best and most effective method for insulation here is foil-coated fiberglass nailed between the studs. This can work very effectively, with the foil facing the interior of the room. But remember, air space between the interior wall and the insulation should be present. That space will capture the warm air and keep it warm within the boundaries of your sauna. A recommended space is about ¾ of an inch between the interior wall and the insulation. Most of the rolled sheets of this type of insulation can be purchased in readily usable sizes—16 inches or 24 inches—so that they will fit nicely between your wall studs.

The common thickness of this fiberglass is between

Walls :   Wall Framing

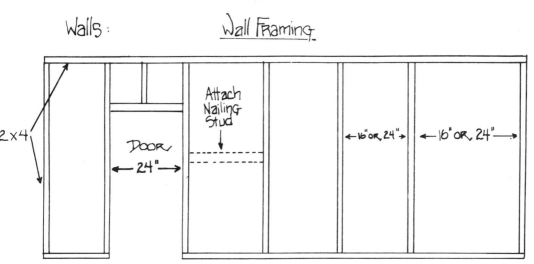

2 x 4

Attach
Nailing
Stud

Door
24"

←16"or 24"→ ←16"or 24"→

The entire unit to be built on floor, then raised, braced, and attached to the Sill Plate.

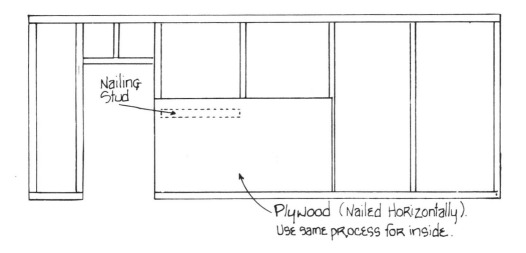

Nailing
Stud

Plywood (Nailed Horizontally).
Use same process for inside.

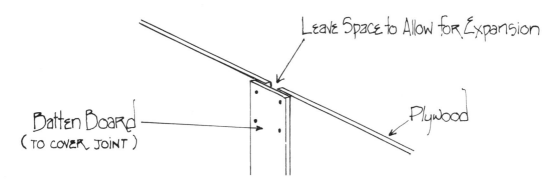

Leave Space to Allow for Expansion

Batten Board
(to cover joint)

Plywood

three and a half and 6 inches. Most builders will recommend that you insulate your roof with a thicker pad than used inside the walls. This is especially true in the stoveroom, where there will be plenty of heat rising to the ceiling and trying to escape.

Other types of insulation, such as the jet-blown plastics, are currently under investigation by federal agencies for their safety factors. They are expensive, and take a professional to install. If you are interested in this type of insulation, merely contact one of your local dealers and ask a few questions. For mere practicality, however, the foil-backed fiberglass insulation is the easiest and most conventional way to insulate your walls and roof. Just staple it against the studs.

Constructing the Walls:

To build a wall is not a complicated matter. But a few logical steps should be taken to avoid problems later on.

The first thing to do is begin with your longest side. The bottom of the wall will be nailed to the sill board along the foundation, and the two walls coming off that wall at right angles will butt into it. So, by starting with the longest one first, you have something to work with.

The easiest way to build a wall is to construct it directly on the foundation itself, with the bottom lined up against the sill board. This will make the job of raising the wall into position quite easy.

A good idea prior to starting construction of a wall is to make a brief sketch of the studs, doorways, etc., and the number of feet between them. This will give you a very good idea of where you are during the actual construction.

Normal distance between studs in a wall is 16 or 24 inches. Most insulation rolls are geared to this measurement, and the job of hanging your insulation will be that much easier with exact measurements.

A wall frame can be quite simple. Using 2 x 4 studs, line up your bottom board and your roof board, then line up your interior studs in a straight vertical configuration. You may use any kind of securing device you choose, from hinge plates to floor nailings. It would be a good idea to discuss with your lumber dealer the best and most secure form of building your frame.

Once the wall is built, you raise it onto the platform or floor itself. Lining up the base board with the sill plate of your floor, you simply nail the wall base into position. Then, using braces, you secure the first wall in place and begin on the next wall. It is advisable to build your exterior walls first, then go inside to divide off your building.

With the walls now in place, you will have a firm foundation for laying the roof.

The Roof

The roof itself can be as simple or difficult a job as you care to make it. Like the initial design of your sauna, however,

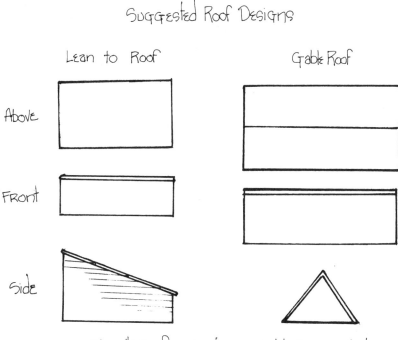

Suggested Roof Designs

Keep the Roof as simple as possible. Be sure that your design includes PITCH for proper drainage.

the roof should be as simple and as effective as possible. One of the vital ingredients of a good sauna roof is its ability to prevent water from seeping into the sauna. Therefore, a roof with a slight angle, or pitch, is preferable. It depends, however, on where you live and how much rainfall or snow you can expect. Notice the angle of cabins in the high mountains—they are dramatically steeped in order to prevent the heavy snow from accumulating on the rooftops. If necessary, give a call to a local builder and ask him what a desirable roof pitch is for your area.

Now, prior to constructing the rafters at the desired pitch, remember a few things about a roof. It must allow for water run-off, and you must make every effort to keep moisture out of your sauna. Eaves extending over the edges of the walls will help dramatically, so figure on a foot or so overhang. And the materials which you choose for your roof must also be weather resistant. Straight plywood nailed directly to the rafters with shingles overlapping downwards and a felt layer between is as good a way as any to stop seepage. To do this, simply nail down the plywood, then attach the strips of felt (15 pound) with the strips running horizontally (keeping water seepage at a minimum) across the roof. To this, you may attach the shingles. Remember to put the shingles on from the lower portions of the roof upwards.

Asphalt shingles are the best and easiest to work with, and with a touch of adhesive or tar beneath each shingle, you have a very secure roof.

Another possibility for the roof is the asphalt roll, which is simply laid on the roof in strips.

Wood shingles, although very pleasing to the eye, are not necessarily the most water resistant of roofings, and should be used only if you are quite sure of the water resistance beneath.

The important thing to remember, however, is that your roof must be as watertight and airtight as possible. Once again, there will be a maximum of heat inside your stoveroom, and you want to keep as much of that heat within the walls as possible. Huge gaps and joints in your roof could prove disastrous to the overall effect of your sauna, so build your roof with care.

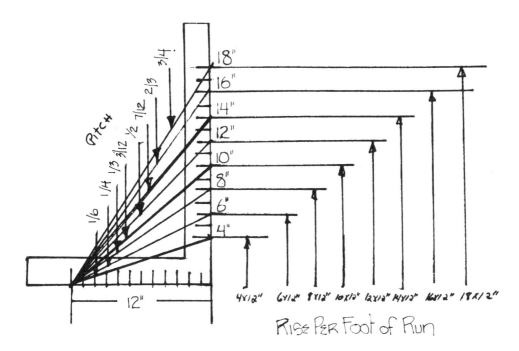

Rise Per Foot of Run

Example: Using a 1/6 pitch the roof will rise 4" per every foot of run.

Roof Structure As Applied to Pitch Scale

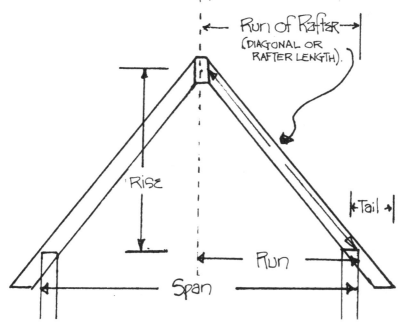

Lean-To Roof:

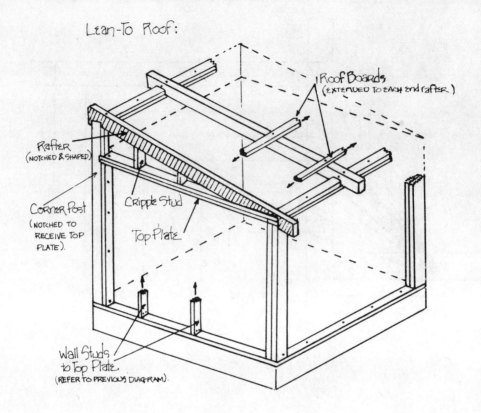

Roof Boards
(EXTENDED TO EACH 2nd rafter.)

Rafter
(NOTCHED & SHAPED)

Corner Post
(NOTCHED TO
RECEIVE TOP
PLATE).

Cripple Stud

Top Plate

Wall Studs
to Top Plate
(REFER TO PREVIOUS DIAGRAM).

Roof Framing Details

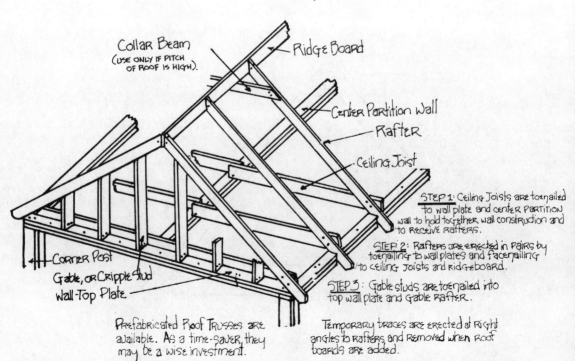

Collar Beam
(USE ONLY IF PITCH
OF ROOF IS HIGH).

Ridge Board

Center Partition Wall

Rafter

Ceiling Joist

Corner Post
Gable, or Cripple Stud
Wall-Top Plate

STEP 1: Ceiling Joists are toenailed
to wall plate and center partition
wall to hold together wall construction and
to receive rafters.

STEP 2: Rafters are erected in pairs by
toenailing to wall plates and facenailing
to ceiling joists and ridgeboard.

STEP 3: Gable studs are toenailed into
top wall plate and gable rafter.

Prefabricated Roof Trusses are
available. As a time-saver, they
may be a wise investment.

Temporary braces are erected at right
angles to rafters and removed when roof
boards are added.

Insulation of the roof, like the walls, should be considered on the basis of humidity and heat preservation. Using the same foil-backed fiberglass, it might be possible to fasten the rolls along the ceiling studs in the interior of your attic, allowing for air space between the actual ceiling and the rolls themselves. Depending upon the height of your roof (the attic space will determine much of your insulation needs here) this might be all the insulation you will need. However, it is best once again to check with your hardware salesman and ask a few questions. He might advise another

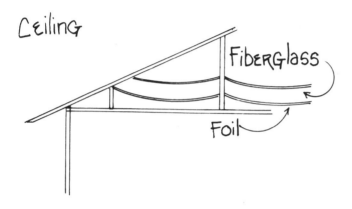

Ceiling

FiberGlass

Foil

Roof:

If there is no attic use heavyweight industrial foil for insulation. If there is an attic use foil-backed insulation, suspended a few inches above the ceiling to create an air pocket.

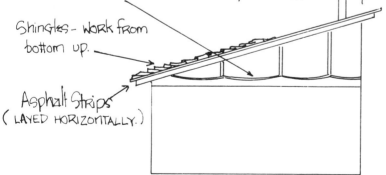

Shingles - work from bottom up.

Asphalt Strips
(LAYED HORIZONTALLY.)

Good angle for water run-off.

roll of foil just beneath the rafters to guarantee proper insulation; or, he might feel that the foil/fiberglass is enough.

Exterior Paneling:

The best covering for the outer walls as well as the inner walls of a sauna is wood. Simply and without argument, wood is the best natural insulator to be found while at the same time being aesthetically pleasing. It is also fairly inexpensive and easy to work with. So, our heartiest recommendation here goes to wood. People have used other materials, however, from tin to sheet metal to other less attractive and less functional materials.

The best and easiest method of covering the outside of your walls is by using plywood sheets. Plywood comes in various widths and lengths, with varying degrees of thickness. The thickness itself is up to you, depending on how sturdy you want your outside walls. The lengths and actual widths should be estimated to fit as snugly into your particular frame size as possible, with the least amount of cutting.

When laying plywood onto a frame, do it horizontally. Make sure the wood stretches as far below the bottom of the floor as possible and that it fits as tightly against the eaves of the roof as possible. This will, once again, guarantee you the best possible insulation and weather protection. You will also be the judge of the number of nailing studs you will need within the frame studs in order to secure your plywood pieces firmly. Nailing studs are normally 2 x 4's, and are secured between the studs. Once the plywood sheets have been nailed to the wall frame, their joints may be covered with a piece of 1 x 2 nailed directly over them. These are called battens, and they are necessary for the weatherproofing and securing of the walls, besides being very attractive.

Remember when applying the plywood to ask your lumber dealer about the expansion of the wood itself. He will probably recommend that you leave a small space between each piece in the joint (this to be covered, of course, by the batten) to allow for eventual expansion of the wood.

The Interior Walls:

The interior of your stoveroom and the quality of wood used is vital to the success of your sauna. The finest grade wood within your budget is a wise investment for a number of reasons. It will be longer lasting, it will seal the room better, and it will not alter its size dramatically under the stress of the hot and cold conditions of your sauna. Remember that the temperature inside your sauna could vary, depending upon where you live, from zero degrees to two hundred degrees when heated. This is a huge amount of temperature variance to ask of any wood, so make sure that the lumber you choose is capable of withstanding these changes.

A chat with your lumber dealer will acquaint you with the various types of wood and their characteristics. Most sauna builders recommend a number of woods for interior use on the walls, as well as the benches of a sauna. These woods are western red cedar, redwood (which is probably the most popular), sugar pine, spruce and aspen. Any of these woods are suitable. And, by investigating the possibilities further with your salesman, you will find that some variations of the lumber are cheaper but will function just as well.

Rough sawn lumber is wood that is coarse on one side, but smooth on the other. This wood, with the rough surface inside and the smooth surface facing the stoveroom, is a cheaper grade than finished lumber and serves the purpose just as well. And, in using this wood for your benches, you will obviously use the rough side as the underside of the seats.

If you tell your lumber salesman exactly what the wood is going to be used for, he will tell you why these kinds of timber are the most acceptable. They are fairly porous, which means they make good insulators. They will not expand or contract as much as other types of wood. And purchased with the fine grade classification, they will not present such problems as knotting or building up sap. Sap, especially, can be disastrous because the juice will boil under the heat of the sauna and drip, causing all kinds of uncomfortable situations. It is recommended that you use a vertical grain, especially for the benches, because that type of wood will not alter its shape as much as a flat grain variety. All in all, it is advisable to use the very best wood inside the stoveroom of a sauna. It is the one room which is going to take a real beating, and you want to maintain its structural stability as well as its beauty. The extra dollars spent on using the best will prove to be a worthwhile investment.

Once you have chosen your wood (with, of course, your insulation in place) you then begin joining the pieces. The two best joints in the world, as proven by our forefathers and builders throughout the ages, for wood that will expand (even the best will move a little) are the tongue and groove joints and the shiplap joints. At this point, also make sure you tell your salesman that you want rust-proof nails, of the finishing quality.

Consider the interior of your sauna a piece of furniture, and nail accordingly. Countersink your nails, blunt the tips to avoid splitting the wood, and don't "overnail" your slats. With the proper grooves, and by nailing each piece at the stud points, you should have a very secure wall.

Doors and Windows:

It's easier to account for the presence of a door prior to sealing in your sauna stoveroom than afterwards, when you yourself are stuck there. Believe it or not, it can happen, and has. And, if desired, consider where you might want a window. Many sauna builders forego the window entirely and use artificial lighting of one type or another in their saunas. But a stained glass window, or one open to the woods, can add a truly lovely effect to your stoveroom.

The easiest and most practical way to build a door is not to build one at all. Rather, purchase one of the hollow wood doors that are lightweight and have good insulation qualities. These doors are easy to manage, and easy to work with.

If you are lucky, you will be able to hang the door directly against a stud, and run support beams across the top to secure the door jamb into its proper position. As we mentioned before, it is much easier if you account for the door's presence during the construction of the wall frame. But even with all the pains taken there, you will find that sometimes the door does not fit exactly. Troubles with hanging doors seem to be axiomatic for all builders, including professionals.

The size of the door is optional. A two-foot width by at least six feet high is a good size, allowing most guests into the stoveroom without problems of a tight squeeze. You don't want to make the door too large, because it will take away from the walking around space of the interior of the stoveroom itself. So, a modestly sized, hollow core door is your best bet.

Ideally, then, you have prepared for the door itself with the stud framing which you have constructed prior to raising the wall. If so, then it's just a matter of hanging the door on three hinges and constructing a stopper at the top of the framework. You have a choice of numerous kinds of handles and stoppers, but remember that the door should close snugly but not be difficult to open. Complicated latchwork is undesirable inside the stoveroom and should be avoided. Also, as we mentioned before in the design chapter of this book, the stoveroom door should always open toward the outside, for safety reasons.

If you must construct a new door frame within the studs of your wall frame, then you have to begin constructing a frame within a frame. Start by measuring the size of your door plus the doorjamb, and erecting what are known as trimmer studs within the wall frame. These will be 2 x 4's and will bring support within the wall frame itself to the doorjamb. Once the trimmer studs are in place, erect a three-sided doorjamb using wood which is wide enough to flush the exterior and interior of your walls. Move the doorjamb into place, using shims wherever needed. Now, you have the essential door configuration ready and you can hang your door.

The insulation of the door itself must be taken into consideration prior to hanging it. By using the same insulation foil as before, attach the stuff to the interior wall of the

Door:

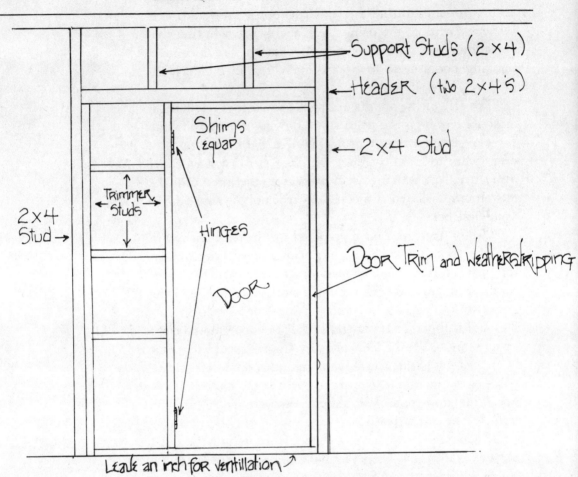

Support Studs (2 × 4)

Header (two 2 × 4's)

Shims (equal)

2 × 4 Stud

Trimmer Studs

2 × 4 Stud →

Hinges

Door Trim and Weatherstripping

Door

Leave an inch for ventillation ↗

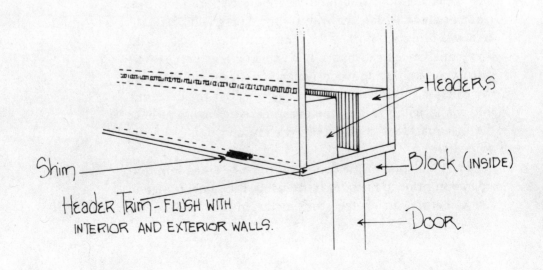

Headers

Shim

Block (inside)

Header Trim - FLUSH WITH INTERIOR AND EXTERIOR WALLS.

Door

door. You can do this with tacks. Then you should cover the inside of the door with the same paneling used on the rest of the wall. This will provide your stoveroom with the proper insulation, and also give the room a coordinated appearance.

If the door does not fit snugly on the door jamb, you may use weather-stripping around the three edges to shut in the heat. Also, at the bottom of the door, you might want to leave about an inch open, which, as we discussed before, will provide for something akin to a ventilation system. And, depending upon the type of platform or foundation you have constructed, you might want to place a piece of wood at the bottom as a door stop, to prevent the door from swinging inward.

One more consideration relating to the door. It is possible that you might consider a window in the door. If so, make sure that you use double sheets of glass for greater insulation. The entire frame including glass should be constructed prior to hanging the door, and fit into the square which you will saw open. However, a window in the door of your sauna provides little benefit and might not be worth the bother. A window placed in the right position on one of the walls, however, might prove to be the most aesthetically pleasing part of your entire sauna.

Door

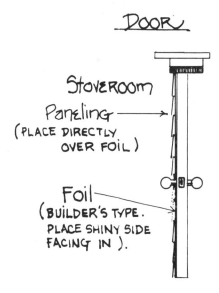

Stoveroom
Paneling ———
(PLACE DIRECTLY
OVER FOIL)

Foil
(BUILDER'S TYPE.
PLACE SHINY SIDE
FACING IN).

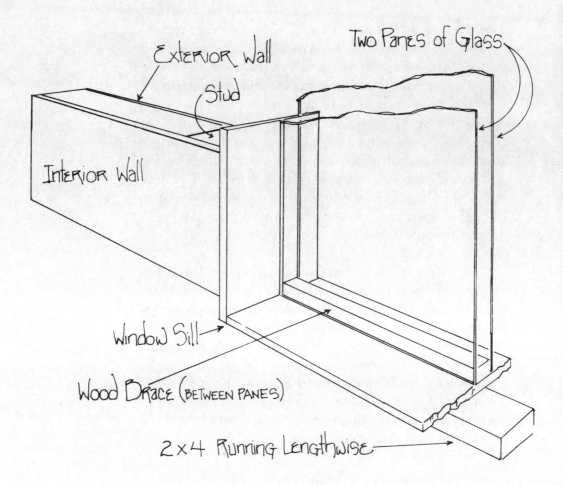

Exterior Wall

Stud

Two Panes of Glass

Interior Wall

Window Sill →

Wood Brace (BETWEEN PANES)

2×4 Running Lengthwise →

As we recommended before, check out your lighting as it comes from the outdoors. You might, if you live in the Northern hemisphere, have a window which faces toward the southwest or directly west. For late afternoon or early evening saunas, the effect of the light entering the stove-room can be tremendous.

As with the door, the decision to insert a window should be made at the time you are constructing your wall frames. The easiest, simplest way of including a window is to make the window frame itself a size that will fit directly and easily into the stud pattern of your wall. A window frame normal-ly consists of a 1 x 2-inch blocking around the glass, with the glass grooved into smaller window blocks. Since it is strongly advisable that you use double plated windows, you will have two panes of glass grooved into the blocks, and that unit then secured to the larger frame.

The window, especially in a sauna, should be of a fairly small size, and once again, should be planned so as to fit between the studs of your wall. This will allow you to secure your window with as little shimmying as possible and thus provide your structure with much more strength.

Prior to fitting the glass into your two block grooves, you might want to consider adding a little artistic touch here and there. I have seen people use a little cement and various colored pieces of plastic or glass to create a beautiful effect within two panes of clear glass. Also, there are those who merely drop a bunch of colored marbles between the panes. Anything that will create a colored panorama when the sunlight shines through will work, and should add an immense amount of beauty to the interior of your stoveroom.

As for the type of glass most suitable for your sauna, you will discover that tempered glass is stronger and more resistant than other commercially sold glass. Once again, it pays to use the finest material possible in this instance, due to the extreme temperatures which will take place within the stoveroom. Your salesman should be able to provide you with the proper glass and fittings for your windows.

Lighting:

Even if you do include a window in the stoveroom of your sauna, you will need another source of light for night time use. The perfect choice among the purists is natural light—either from the wood burning in the stove or, simply, from a candle. Anyone who has ever lit a room by candlelight knows how beautiful and serene the room becomes, and this is the perfect atmosphere for a sauna. A few well-placed candles will do extremely nice things for your stoveroom.

Electrical lighting inside the stoveroom is popular with some people. However, the process of installing wires and passing the electrical codes can be bothersome and aggravating. I will not suggest means of installing electricity in your stoveroom, because of the wealth of codes and the potential for hazard. The best way to go about it is to hire an electrician, get inspected, and flick on the switch.

Probably the worst kind of lighting to use is gas or kerosene. These are volatile materials, and if spilled, are hazardous. Do not, on any account, use propane. You will notice on each can of the compressed gas a warning about maximum temperature exposures. An exploding can of propane in your sauna can put a quick and dangerous end to a beautiful evening. Once again, candles are cheap, and much safer.

With a properly placed window to capture the sun, and one or two candles for night lighting, you can illuminate your sauna in a natural and romantic fashion.

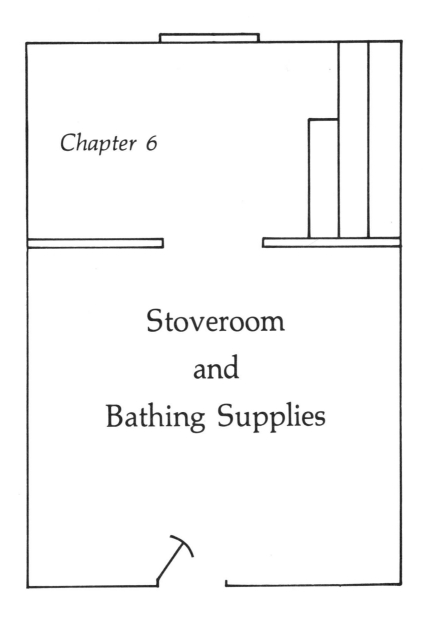

Chapter 6

Stoveroom
and
Bathing Supplies

NOW THAT THE BASIC SHELL of your sauna has been completed and the inner walls secured, the next step is to deal with the stoveroom and its facilities. By these we mean the stove itself, the benches, the rocks and any other accoutrements you may care to add to your sauna.

The Stove:

Prior to the arrival of the industrial age, saunas were heated by wood burning stoves. For centuries the Finns used a simple version of the common Ben Franklin potbelly, of various shapes and sizes but with the same effect. The rocks were put on the top grill, with a bucket of water nearby and a ladle to create steam by pouring the water onto the rocks. The ultimate simplicity of this system makes it a popular favorite even today. The purists throughout the world emphasize the traditional nature of the wood burning stove, as well as other advantages such as the sound of logs crackling in the burner, the sweet smell of burning wood, and the

Gas Sauna Heaters:

Typical heater from Finno Corporation

Through the wall vent

Typical Electric Sauna Heater

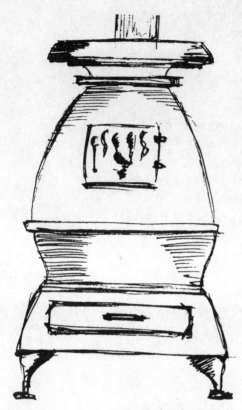

A Classical Wood-Burning Stove

simplicity of using such a stove without the hassles of permits and inspections.

The Industrial Age, however, brought some new and very fine ways to heat a sauna. The electrical stove and the gas burning stove are the two most widely used systems outside the wood burning stove. They do possess some benefits which are absent from the wood stove. They are clean, do not demand the carrying of wood and the stockpiling of wood, and are usually lighter and easier to install than the wood burning stove. Yet, with all their advantages, the gas and electric stoves have taken a second place to the wood burning stove for heating saunas.

No matter which type of stove you choose, however, you will find problems and circumstances which you must plan for prior to installation.

There are now many companies in existence which produce electrical sauna heaters at very reasonable prices. (A partial list is given in Appendix A.). Their heaters are, on the whole, economical, sturdy and quite efficient. They are clean burning and do not require the space for wood that a wood burning unit does. The only problems with an electrical heater is installation of the unit itself. Because most heaters work on a high voltage system, you will most likely have to hire an electrician to install your wiring. Also, most new electrical wiring must be inspected by an official from your area. The adherents of the electrical stove enjoy their product because of its simple operation—just flick a switch and let it heat up—and because of the cleanliness of the unit.

Also remember that with an electrical stove, even though you don't need a chimney, you should still provide for some kind of ventilation system. The design we suggested earlier in the book—your intake from below and behind the stove and your outlet at the highest point near the ceiling and to the rear of the stoveroom—is probably the most effective system to use for ventilating when using an electrical stove. Just remember that ventilation is important no matter what kind of heating unit you use.

The gas stove has its useful points also. The fact that in some places wood is difficult to obtain, or electricity is impossible to install might prompt the sauna owner to install a gas stove. It all depends on how much trouble you want to take with your stove, and whether hauling bottles of gas back and forth is a reasonable way to fuel your sauna.

When installing your gas stove, remember that it will be necessary to have a flue, and that you will have to take this into consideration during the early stages of the sauna's construction.

And finally, there is the wood stove. These come in all shapes and sizes from old fashioned potbelly models to modern, functional square stoves. Most manufacturers of wood burning stoves, as well as those who manufacture the electrical and gas stoves, will provide you with the proper information as to the size of your unit. Obviously, larger stoverooms need more heat, and thus, a larger stove. The manufacturers have converted the energy output of their products into everyday language of square and cubic foot dimensions. So, these are fine guidelines to follow.

If your decision is to use a wood burning stove, you will have to consider insulation and fireproofing on the floor beneath the stove and in the walls behind it. The best fireproofing in the world is distance. In other words, keep the stove away from walls as much as possible. This factor will have to be considered in your design stage.

Asbestos is the best fireproofing material available. You can purchase it as board or in cement strips. On the wall directly behind your stove, you might consider erecting an asbestos wall, made out of the cement strips. This is simply done by blocking the board out from the wall about two inches, thus leaving the protective wall directly behind the stove, and an air pocket between the wall and your stove-room wall. The size of the wall should be determined by the size of your stove and the room which you have available for your stove. The wall, however, should be at least a foot larger than the stove on either side.

On the floor beneath the stove itself, you have a variety of choices for fireproofing. Bricks are very beautiful, easy to work with, and provide an excellent stove pad. You may also use concrete, gravel or cement blocks, depending upon your finances and tastes. But do not set the stove directly on the floor. The combination of the weight and the heat will almost certainly damage a plywood base and could prove dangerous.

If you are going to use the wood burning stove, you must also consider a chimney. The proper size of the chimney will most likely be provided by the manufacturer—a size that will carry the smoke away as well as generating enough of an updraft to keep the fire burning hot inside the stove. It would be wise to determine where that chimney will go—either through the roof or through the walls of the stoveroom—before ordering it.

If you decide to take the chimney through the roof, you will have to deal with the problem of sealing the roof and cutting off any possible leaks as a result of the hole. The process is rather time consuming and expensive.

Through the wall, however, you do not run the risk of leakage, and by sending the chimney out through a level opening, then angling it upwards, you must concern your-self only with a vertical cut in the wall. This eliminates much work on the roof and the ceiling and is easier to attach, since all you will need are braces to secure the chimney against the outer wall.

You will also have to consider the type of chimney you want to install. There are three varieties of chimneys now on the market—the single wall, the double wall, and the triple wall. Cheaper and lighter, the single wall chimney has its drawbacks because it does not hold the heat as well as the other two. Also, it will become very hot to the touch. (Asbestos around the chimney where it passes through the wall or roof will eliminate the danger of heat there). The double and triple walled chimneys are good because they retain the heat, keeping the outer surface cooler, and providing good insulation.

If you decide to run the chimney through the wall, you will want some metal surface to pass the pipe through. The one with the lowest conductivity of heat is tin, and by taking a square piece and cutting a hole in it, you have perfect passage through the wall. Leave some space around the chimney pipe for air, and as we mentioned before, some asbestos around the pipe at this point is not a bad idea.

At the top of the chimney, you should put a rain cap to prevent water from dripping on down and dousing your fire. If you purchase your stove and chimney from a manufacturer, the cap will be included.

Remember when installing your chimney that no matter what grade you use, there will always be some heat emanating from the surface. Keep the pipes at all times at least nine inches from the surface of the wood; do not allow your chimney to touch the walls at any point.

If you are going to use a wood burning stove in your sauna, then obviously you will want to consider the kind of wood best suited to the sauna. The wood should be dense so it will burn more efficiently. It should also be dry, with as little sap as possible. Dead trees are very good for this because the sap was not running through the trees at the time of cutting. When burning the wood, smaller logs are preferable, since they burn hotter.

The worst fuel to burn for a sauna fire are the soft

The Nippa WB Model may be used for both "original" water heating arrangements, or to heat water in pressure tanks. Commercially cast grates and ash pan are included. *Picture courtesy of Bruce Manufacturing Company, Bruce Crossing, Michigan.*

woods, like pine and aspen. They go up fast and do little more than provide an exciting flame. Some of the best woods are the heaviest and densest, like elm, oak and beech.

When stockpiling your wood, remember that the best wood is dry, dead wood that has no sap or moisture. You will want to keep the wood on an elevated surface to prevent ground moisture from coming in contact with it. And, you will want to make sure that there is a good passage of air through your stockpile. Wood clumped together in neatly stacked piles with no air passage becomes a fine environment for the production of mildew and moss, definitely undesirable forms of life on the wood which you will use in your stove.

The Metos Wall Heater saves space and makes cleaning the floor easier. The tubular heating elements are hermetically sealed. Wall heaters are recommended for rooms up to 650 cubic feet. *Picture courtesy of Metos Sauna, Inc., Bellevue, Michigan.*

Keep in mind also that no matter how dry you might keep the heat inside your stoveroom, there will almost always be some humidity present. So, do not stockpile your wood in the stoveroom. When designing your sauna, remember to keep the woodpile away from any water sources, such as the tank or shower room. A storage room separate from these sources of humidity is a good idea, or even placing the woodpile in the dressing room will work.

The Metos Floor Heater, like the Wall Heater, features triple air chambers made of non-corrosive metals. It also features an overhead safety switch. Designed for sauna rooms of up to 1,150 cubic feet, it is available in five different models. *Picture courtesy of Metos Sauna, Inc., Bellevue, Michigan.*

The Nippa WC model is ideal for use with wood, coal, or coke. It is equipped with a direct heating water tank as shown in the illustration. Its advantage is the speed with which it heats water. It holds 125 pounds of rock as compared to the WB model capacity of 150 pounds. *Picture courtesy of Bruce Manufacturing Company, Bruce Crossing, Michigan.*

The Benches:

The proper kind of wood must also be chosen for the benches within the stoveroom. The benches are extremely important because you and your guests will spend plenty of time reclining and sitting on them. Therefore, when considering the kind of wood best suited to the bench, you must

Stoves and Chimneys:

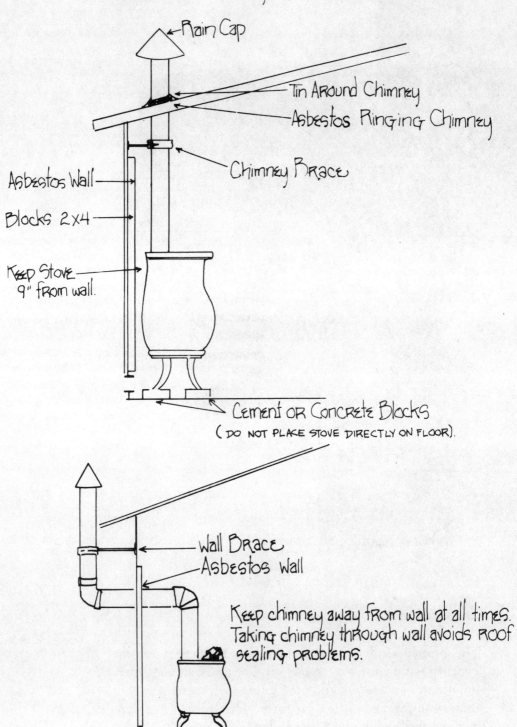

Rain Cap

Tin Around Chimney

Asbestos Ringing Chimney

Chimney Brace

Asbestos Wall

Blocks 2x4

Keep Stove
9" from wall.

Cement or Concrete Blocks
(DO NOT PLACE STOVE DIRECTLY ON FLOOR).

Wall Brace
Asbestos Wall

Keep chimney away from wall at all times.
Taking chimney through wall avoids roof
sealing problems.

take into account the heat factor, the grain, the potential for splinters and the durability of the wood which you choose.

Purists of the sauna have a favorite wood—redwood. They claim that it remains cool, is easy to work with, and generally gives the sauna a beautiful appearance. Cedar and sugar pine are also acceptable woods, but not as popular as redwood.

In choosing wood for your benches, you should watch for impurities in the lumber, such as sap and rough edges, which could prove harmful under the extreme conditions of heat which you will experience in the stoveroom. Rough-edged wood, however, can be overcome by using cocomats or even towels. Many people prefer the use of towels on their benches because of their absorbency.

Benches are extremely versatile, and may be constructed to almost any design you wish. There are, however, factors which you should keep in mind when designing the actual layout for your benches. The width of the benches should be of a dimension that allows for comfortable reclining or sitting. A good figure for this width is two feet. That will provide enough space for the average sized man to recline comfortably without falling off the edges. The height of the bench is also optional, and often can be calculated merely by dangling your legs and measuring the height needed. A good estimate would be between a foot and two feet high. The length of your bench depends upon the length of your stoveroom. Remember that you should minimize the empty space and use your cubic feet in such a manner as to provide the greatest amount of bench space possible. So benches reaching wall to wall are desirable.

You will probably want your benches designed in a step pattern, with possibly three levels reaching to a height of no more than three and a half feet from the ceiling. By simply drawing a diagram, mapping out the width and the height of each step, you should be able to determine easily just where your steps will go. Of course, you can use a multitude of variations on the step theme—having the lower step wide for reclining, or, having the upper berth the widest. It's up to you. Just remember that the heat in the stoveroom rises, and the top step will receive the greatest amount of sauna heat.

Basic Bench Design

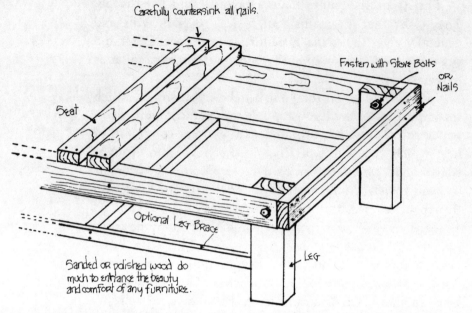

Carefully countersink all nails.

Fasten with Stove Bolts
OR
Nails

Seat

Optional Leg Brace

LEG

Sanded or polished wood do
much to enhance the beauty
and comfort of any furniture.

A Combination of Benches:

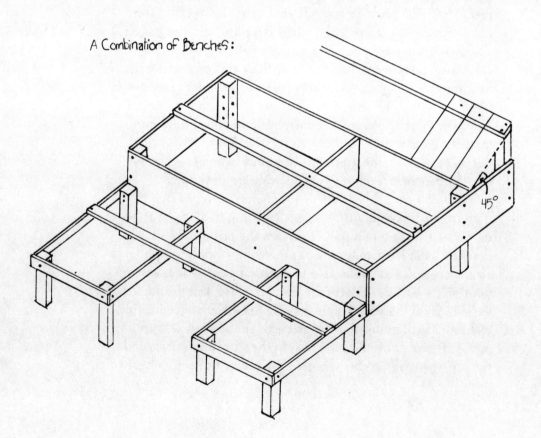

45°

Some of the diagrams included here will show the basic elements of constructing a bench and provide some designs you might want to use.

Bathing Supplies:

The sauna traditionally involves much more than just sitting in the stoveroom and heating up. As integral and important to the success of a sauna is the total immersion of the bather in cold water. To many, this is the peak of a sauna, the moment when it all comes together. The pores of the skin have been opened as the bather sits in the heat of the stoveroom, and the sudden immersion into cold water slams these pores shut.

The water source which creates this magical moment is all important. As we discussed before, in brief, a shower is a passable substitute for a water tank. And redwood tubs, or even a regular tub, can be used. But, if at all possible, you will want to create a water source whereby the bather can literally plunge himself into the tank in one quick movement.

There are a number of ways of securing a water tank. You may purchase a commercial tank from a manufacturer. You may buy a used water tank at a sale. Or, you may make your own. But the construction of a water tank is so difficult that we advise you to purchase one.

One of the best alternatives to a tank is the backyard plastic pool. Relatively inexpensive and available in a multitude of shapes and sizes, it can work very effectively as an immersion tank. These pools are easy to install, easy to maintain, and provide total immersion. The plastic pool can at least be used in the warmer months, with a simple shower filling in for the rest.

As time goes by, you might want to consider a more permanent water tank, such as a redwood tub. For the time being, however, just keep in mind the dimensions which are necessary to make the water tank an effective part of your sauna. You will want it deep enough for the plunge, and wide enough for an average man to stretch out in. Some-

Benches:

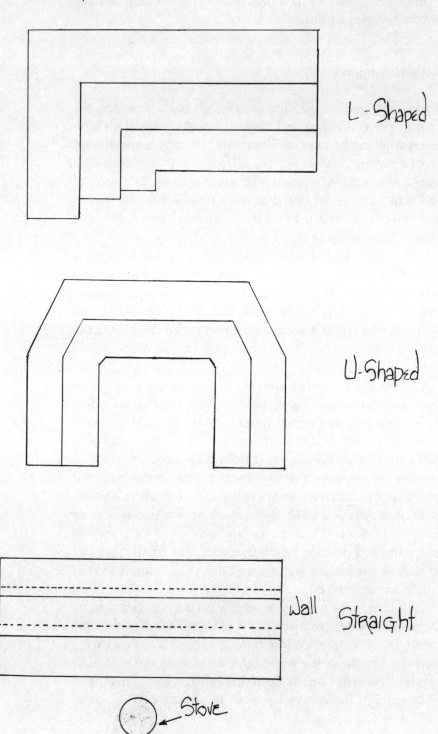

L-Shaped

U-Shaped

Wall

Wall Straight

Stove

thing around six feet across with a depth of four feet should accommodate your needs very well.

Stoveroom Accessories:

The little things necessary for a good sauna should become obvious as you prepare to ready your building for use: clothes hangers, towel racks, benches as needed throughout the building, other windows, etc. Inside the stoveroom, however, there are a few more additions that are absolutely necessary.

First, you will need a water bucket. Preferably, the

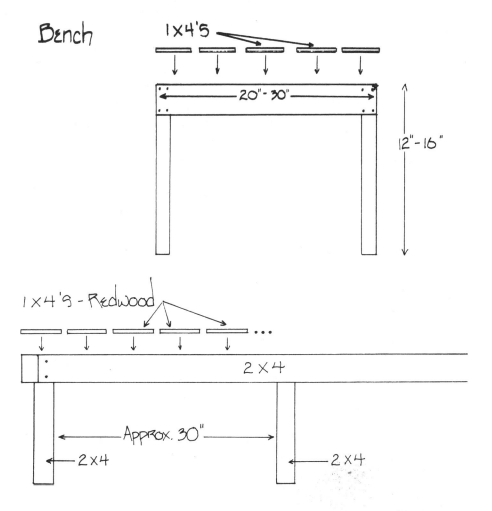

bucket should be made of wood and should be leakproof. Petroleum products such as plastic are undesirable because of their tendency to melt. You will also need a ladle, also preferably made out of wood, to pour the water onto the rocks. In your initial design of the stoveroom, the water bucket should be accounted for. You do not want to have to keep running out of the stoveroom for more water during your sauna.

The rocks which you will be using must have certain qualities because of the heat stress they will undergo. The Finns use a rock which they call *konno*; supposedly this rock comes from the lava flow of a huge volcano somewhere in Finland. The rocks are extremely popular because they hold the heat without cracking and splitting. If you have ever built a fire pit with rock, you know how unpleasant cracking rocks can be. Not only unpleasant, but somewhat dangerous as the rocks tend to explode and send chips flying off in all directions. The *konno* rock is a *peridotite malm*, and is sold commercially. If these stones are not available in your neighborhood, you might want to check with your local quarry or speak to a mineralogist about the best rocks which are available. Remember, you want stones that do not crack and which hold the heat well.

Care of the Stoveroom:

Once your stoveroom has been completed, there are a number of things which should be done to guarantee the beauty and health of that room for the years to come. The first of these is the curing of the room immediately following the final phase of construction. This process rids the stoveroom of the shavings, scraps and debris left over from construction. It is important for the stoveroom to be as clean as possible because anything left around, like bits of wood, might very well incinerate under the terrific heat of the sauna once the stoveroom is put into operation.

The first step in curing a stoveroom involves a general clean-up. Sweep up the scraps left on the floor, and remove any pieces of wood and other materials that do not belong. Secondly, wash down the wood interior, the benches, etc., with a damp cloth. Third, wipe off the sauna rocks themselves, cleaning them of any dirt or packaging debris which might be left on them.

If you have purchased an electric heater, it is advisable to cure the heater also. Do this simply by turning the heater on and allowing it to heat the stoveroom to the customary 180 degrees. Any packaging debris left on the heater itself will burn off in the process, perhaps creating smoke. But this will prevent any unpleasantness during an actual sauna in the future.

Another process which you might consider for your stoveroom is one which is known as chemical staining. The Finnish Building Standards Institute recommends a procedure which is safe, effective and long lasting. The staining process will provide the interior of your sauna with a beautiful sheen and texture.

The first step in this process is to dry the stoveroom out if it has been in use. Then, sand down all the wooden surfaces, thus readying them for the eventual staining. The metal work inside should be protected with a covering once the stoveroom has been cleaned.

Now, apply a chemical known as pyrogallic acid in a three to five percent solution. Pyrogallic acid is used by photographers in their development processes and should be readily available at any camera supply store. Using a brush, apply the solution to the wood surfaces evenly. Once this is completed, secure the room and make it airtight.

The next step is to place about a quart of ammonia solution (35 to 40 percent) in a bowl in the center of the storeroom and allow the solution to evaporate. You can speed up the evaporation process by turning on the heat. Allow approximately a half hour for the evaporation to occur. Remember, ammonia is a poisonous gas, so once you have begun this procedure, seal the room and leave it. Do not stand around waiting to see the results.

Once the ammonia has evaporated, open the room and circulate the air. Your walls should now have a darkened stain and a lovely sheen. If the stain is not quite up to what you had expected, you can repeat the process a number of times until the desired gloss is obtained.

Once this staining process has been completed to your

satisfaction, you will never have to repeat it again. Your sauna should retain the sheen and the hue forever. Of course, if you do not want to bother with the process at the outset, you can always do it at a later time. The only requirement is that your sauna be dry and clean to begin with.

Caring for your sauna once you have begun to use it is a rather simple process. General scrubbing and hosing down should be sufficient to keep the wood clean and the surfaces sanitary. Remember, people will be perspiring quite a bit on the wood, and cleanliness here is an imperative. It is best to wash the stoveroom out at least once after every sauna. It is also important to keep the room aired and dry. Wood will rot eventually under humid conditions, but by a continual process of airing out the room, you should be able to avoid that problem.

Remember that the sauna is traditionally a clean and healthy undertaking, and no one enjoys walking into a messy, mouldy environment for such an activity. It will greatly increase the pleasure of your sauna baths if the surroundings are hygienic and well cared for.

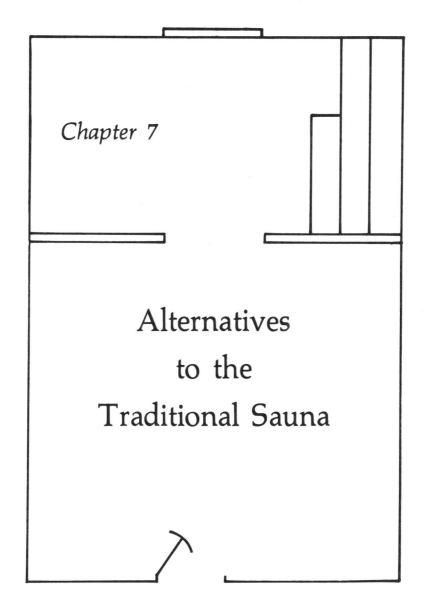

Chapter 7

Alternatives
to the
Traditional Sauna

IN GIVING INSTRUCTIONS on how to construct a sauna on a piece of property, this book has so far neglected city-dwellers, apartment residents, and occupants of homes with little or no property who wish to erect a sauna. Well, there's no need to give up the idea of having your own sauna because you think you lack space. If you presently live in a home with little or no property, or reside in an apartment, there are ways to overcome these limitations.

Basement Saunas:

The best and easiest solution to the lack of space for a sauna is if you happen to live in a home which has a basement. Most of these are large enough to accommodate at least a fair sized stoveroom, and actually make the construction of that room easier because of the already existing walls.

The typical basement has a concrete floor and concrete walls with heating and water pipes running overhead. It is usually squared off at the corners, with enough ceiling clearance to construct a six or seven-foot wall. So, using this typical basement structure, let's proceed with the steps necessary to erect a stoveroom beneath your home.

First, of course, you lay out the floor plan. The fact that you already possess a concrete floor helps, because you will not have to lay a foundation. Instead, you can lay your sill plates directly onto the concrete, using masonry bolts or ram-set guns. We assume here that you will be utilizing the two existing corner walls of the basement—this is the simplest and most practical method of building.

Once the sill plates have been secured, you may then begin constructing your walls using the same platform techniques described earlier. The difference here will be the concrete walls of the basement itself. Instead of framing a wall and then raising it, you will simply secure furring strips onto the concrete for nailing horizontally or vertically, depending upon which way you want to panel the interior of the sauna. Once again, use masonry nails. If you nail vertical strips along the concrete wall, it is advisable to keep them 16 inches apart on center. The insulation which you will place between the strips will fit snugly with this dimension.

Now, prior to raising the two new walls, it will be necessary to think in terms of the floor. A hanging joist system, using stirrups, is good here because it allows you to drop some polyethylene plastic between the joists to create a vapor shield. Make sure that the drainage here is also suitable—most basement floors already have a pitch specifically designed for drainage purposes. But allow for water seepage through the plastic and the joists onto the concrete itself and make sure that the pitch goes in the direction of your basement drain. If this ideal situation does not exist, a little touch of refinishing of your concrete floor will help.

Now, the floor is secured, using plywood boards, wood strips, or even duckboards over the joists. Raise the 2 x 4 walls into position and secure them to the sill plates. Remember to secure nailing studs to the basement's concrete walls where your walls will butt, and provide a nailing stud for your sill plate where it butts into the concrete. By using the two already existing walls, you will only have to be certain that your sill plates are secure to achieve a sturdy frame.

In framing your walls, it is important to take into consideration the height. Most basements have pipes running overhead, and it is vital that you do not include the pipes inside your stoveroom. So, the ceiling must run lower than the pipes, and, any pipes which run directly over the stoveroom itself must be insulated properly. There will be an intense amount of heat escaping from the sauna, and that heat could affect your pipes badly.

The ceiling itself is a simplified version of the simple lean-to style, only it can be flat. Since you will not be competing with outside weather conditions, it is not necessary to build the ceiling with a pitch, or angle. So, by using a simple construction of rafters with insulation between the interior paneling and the upper paneling, and providing enough space for the vapor hold, you should have little trouble constructing a simple, workable ceiling.

Once the walls and ceiling are in place, refer to Chapter 6 concerning the placement and insulation of the stove, making sure once again that you take all the precautions necessary to fireproof that area. Ventilation inside the basement may be a problem. But if you use forethought in determining exactly where you are going to construct the sauna, you might avoid that problem.

Using an already existing ventilation pipe, for instance, one that runs from your furnace, would be a simple and practical solution to ridding your stoveroom of the chimney's smoke. But for most people, this problem does not exist because they have come to the very practical conclusion that using an electrical heater inside the home sauna is far superior to using a wood burning stove. The electrical heater is simple, clean and efficient. It does not necessitate the storing of wood for burning, and finally, does not require a flue.

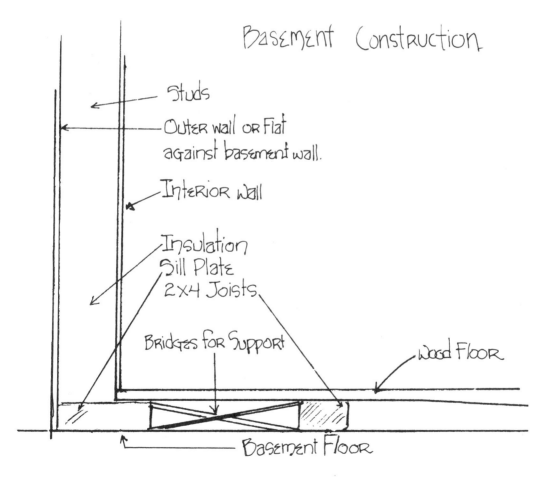

As for the simple ventilation problems themselves, often the basement area can be used in the same manner in which outdoor ventilation is used by means of an intake opening near the stove, and an outlet vent high on the wall at the farthest point from the intake. If your basement sauna happens to be near a window, you might want to construct a ventilation system that uses fresh air instead of basement air.

The remaining qualities of the sauna itself are quite similar to those of an outdoor sauna. The difference with the basement sauna, in simple terms, is the presence of two walls and the absence of weather. Otherwise, the other conditions which exist for an outdoor sauna also exist for a basement sauna.

One note here: if you desire a basement sauna and don't feel up to the handyman, do-it-yourself routine, you might want to check the list of custom sauna companies at the end of this book. There are a number of them, and they can supply you with a prefabricated sauna—two foot by four foot pieces of wall which interlock and can be assembled easily and quickly. These prefabricated saunas, since they are of modular design, can be adapted to any size you need.

Mini-Saunas:

Many apartment dwellers and home owners without basements are discovering the miracle of the miniature sauna designed for the hallway or small nook just outside the bathroom. There are a number of companies which specialize in small, compact models designed specifically for the apartment or home. They are easy to assemble and easy to take apart, so you may carry them with you when you move.

The best way to go about getting the right sauna for your particular needs is to write to the companies listed in the back of this book, explain your needs, and see what they have to offer. Of course, this is not a total do-it-yourself job, but in some cases, the prefabricated modular stoverooms are the most practical answer.

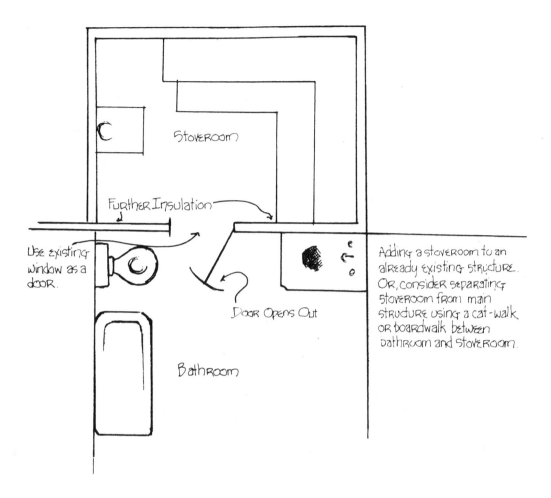

Use existing window as a door.

Further Insulation

Stoveroom

Door Opens Out

Bathroom

Adding a stoveroom to an already existing structure. Or, consider separating stoveroom from main structure using a cat-walk or boardwalk between bathroom and stoveroom.

Attaching a Sauna to Your Home:

Even people who own their homes find themselves with backyards which are just too small to accommodate a full sauna, complete with dressing room, storage room, deck and all the other elements which go to make up a complete sauna system. For these people, there are some very practical ways of utilizing what already exists to create a full sauna.

In doing this, you will be concerned only with the building of the stoveroom as an addition to your home. And you will most likely place that stoveroom nearest the most convenient room, the bathroom, for your sauna activities.

Take a look at your home, and you will probably discover that the bathroom wall faces out into the backyard. You will probably also notice that the wall contains an open space large enough for a door. By cutting an opening into this wall (if there is a window there, all the better) and adding the stoveroom onto the outside of your bathroom, you will have created a sauna in which the bathroom will act as dressing and shower rooms.

Probably the simplest way to go about designing such a room is to consider leaving a space between the stoveroom wall and the bathroom wall. This allows you to remain consistent with your walls of the stoveroom, and will probably provide better insulation once the walls are up.

The diagram on page 109 is a good example of how to

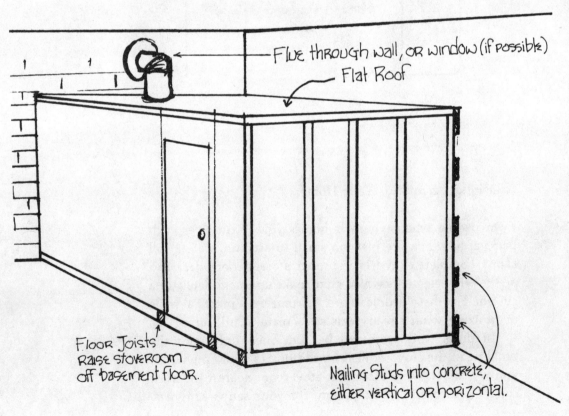

The Basement Sauna

Flue through wall, or window (if possible)

Flat Roof

Floor Joists raise stoveroom off basement floor.

Nailing Studs into concrete, either vertical or horizontal.

structure such an addition. The same methods apply here as for the outdoor sauna, only now you must consider breaking through the bathroom wall and constructing a door there which will lead outside to the stoveroom. Other niceties which may be considered are canopies over the walkway for privacy, and wind shield walls on either side for the comfort of your sauna bathers as they return to the shower.

In building such an addition, you will lessen the overall expense of your sauna by utilizing the plumbing already found in the bathroom. Your only concern is that of the stoveroom; everything else is already there. Also, for people with space limitations, this solution is highly recommended. An eight by ten-foot stoveroom will not take up any more space than a normal sized storage shed. If your backyard already has a swimming pool, you will have to consider this space-saving solution seriously.

A backyard swimming pool can be used as your submersion tank simply by leaving one side of the walkway exposed with steps leading to the pool. This would allow your bathers to leave the sauna, submerge themselves in the pool, then return to the bathroom or dressing room. As for a relaxation room, your den or living room can easily be used.

In other words, look at your home, your available space and your financial limitations, and improvise a little in the construction of your stoveroom. You might find, even if you do have the space, that such an arrangement might be preferable to the construction of an entire sauna system in the backyard.

Another aspect of the sauna made for the apartment or small backyard is the size. Many companies produce saunas which are geared for just one person. Now, if you're the type who enjoys solitude, then the one bather cubicle would be just your style. But if you enjoy sharing the pleasure of sauna with your spouse and friends, then you'd better opt for a larger unit.

With the small sauna designed for the interior of the home or apartment, the use of electric heaters is highly recommended. The traditionalists may scoff at this, preferring a wood burning stove or nothing at all. But the electric heaters, especially in such a small area, are definitely more practical. There is no need to store wood, no need to consider the installation of a flue, and no mess or fuss. A wood burning stove would be highly impractical in this environment and you should think twice before making a decision to use one.

The sauna is an experience which you will enjoy through the years, no matter where or how you live. Even if you don't own wooded acreage with a convenient lakefront a few yards from your front door, or if you don't have a home with a spacious backyard waiting for a sauna building, do not be discouraged. The sauna experience can be tailored to your needs and a small, modern one can provide as much enjoyment and healthful benefit as a large traditional type.

Appendix A

Manufacturers of Sauna Equipment

Am-Finn Sauna
7th and Washington Streets
Red Hill, Pennsylvania 18076

Am-Finn specializes in the production of prefabricated stoverooms, ready to assemble. Their designs range from a 4 x 4 to an 8 x 10 model.

Am-Finn also builds and sells heaters, complete with all the electrical paraphernalia needed for a hook-up.

Beehive Sauna
3222 North Marks Ave.
Fresno, California 93705

Beehive Sauna specializes in prefabricated stoverooms with a unique construction design using a honeycombed pattern which makes excellent use of air as an insulator. Their sizes range from a 4 x 5 to an 8 x 8. The price for the average stoveroom is in the area of $1,800. A full price list will be supplied by the manufacturer.

Cecil Ellis Sauna Corporation
Powder Hill
P.O. Box 204
Middlefield, Connecticut 06455

Cecil Ellis Sauna Corporation is one of the foremost producers of saunas in the world. They specialize in stoverooms ranging from 4 x 3 to a large 12 x 12 size. They will also negotiate on custom designed stoverooms for a particular need.

Custom Sauna
4368 Hayman Ave.
La Canada, California 91011

Custom Sauna is the major importer for Tume Sauna rooms in the United States. The Tume stoveroom is the

115

standard modular design, and comes in a variation of sizes. Custom Sauna also handles Metos heaters.

Erik Sauna
Baths International, Inc.
101 Park Ave.
New York City, New York 10017

Erik Sauna deals in a wide range of prefabricated stoverooms and specializes in custom built rooms to your specifications. Their sizes vary from a 3 x 4 model to a 10 x 12 unit. They also distribute Helo stoves, one of the more popular brands of heaters used in saunas today.

Finno Co.
15836 Lahey St.
Granada Hills, California 91344

The Finno Company deals in gas heaters, supplying along with those heaters vent systems and accessories necessary for installation.

Metos Sauna, Inc.
13000 Bellevue Redmond Rd.
Bellevue, Washington 98005

Metos Sauna is one of the largest producers of the complete sauna in the world. Along with their electric heaters, which are highly recommended, they also produce modular stoveroom units designed primarily for installation indoors. They range in size from 4 x 6 to 8 x 10. Metos also deals in the electrical components such as thermostats, control panels and contactors necessary for the function of electrical heaters.

NIPPA Sauna Heaters
Bruce Manufacturing Company
Bruce Crossing, Michigan 49912

For a wood-burning stove, NIPPA Sauna is the place to go. They are the foremost producers of such stoves. They also manufacture gas and electric heaters, as well as a full line of thermostats and other accessories for the stoveroom.

Sauna Distributors, Inc.
MacLevy Products Corp.
92-21 Corona Ave.
Elmhurst, New York 11373

Sauna Distributors is basically the distribution agent for Helo products, which is one of the largest builders of sauna heaters in the world. Sauna Distributors also sells a number of prefabricated models of stoverooms ranging from a 3 x 4 model to a large 10 x 12.

Toivo Sauna Heaters
Micro Metals, Inc.
1000 Levee St.
P.O. Box 192
Red Wing, Minnesota 55066

Toivo specializes in electric heaters, with some of very unique design. They also sell stoverooms in various sizes and models.

Ultra Sauna
Vico Products Manufacturing Co., Inc.
1808 Patrera Ave.
South El Monte, California 91733

Vico Products builds and sells electric and gas heaters for the sauna. Also, they produce a line of stoverooms, and will do some amount of custom work.

Viking Sauna Co.
909 Park Ave.
P.O. Box 6298
San Jose, California 95150

Viking is a very large and very well known producer and importer of sauna heaters and rooms. Their specialty is the electric heater. They also manufacture stoverooms, and will do custom work.

Appendix B

General Price List of Materials (for the Construction of one 8 x 10 Sauna)

1. *Using Post-Beam Foundation:*
   A. Post or concrete, approximately $10.00.
   B. Railroad ties for beams @ $7.77 per beam = $31.08.
   C. Clamps, etc. $10.00.

   TOTAL: $51.00

   Note: This figure does not include the rental of tools such as post-hole diggers, etc.

2. *Supplies for Wall Framing and Floor Construction:*
   A. Using 2 x 4 redwood stud grade, you will need approximately 600 lineal feet. At an average cost of $ .35 per lineal foot, this works out to an estimated $210.00 for your stud needs.
   B. Plywood for use on the walls, both inside and out, the celing and the floor amounts to approximately 420 sq. ft. Plywood sells for $18.00 per 32 sq. ft. (shop grade, ¾ inch and in 4 x 8 ft. sheets). You will need approximately 13 sheets which comes to a price of $234.00.

   TOTAL: $444.00

3. *The Roof:*
   A. Plywood — 3 pieces @ $18.00 per is $54.00.
   B. Asphalt shingles (USG Corp.) — 50 lineal ft. for $15.00 (9 x 12 shingles) — considering the overlap, a hundred lineal feet should do it. = $30.00.
   C. Felt rolls — approximately $10.00.

   TOTAL: $94.00

4. *Paneling and Trim:*
A. Using redwood 1 x 12 x 8, at a cost of approximately $6.00 per board, you will use approximately 80 or so boards to panel the interior and exterior of your sauna. Of course, the grade of wood need not be so expensive (check chapter on lumber) = $380.00.
B. Trim, etc., is difficult to estimate depending upon what your tastes and requirements are. But figure at least another $100.00 into your budget for excess wood.

TOTAL: $480.00

5. *Other Needs:*
A. The stove: the prices range incredibly from $25.00 for an old wood stove to $500.00 for an electric with all the controls.
B. Benches: depending upon how much and how large. The cost, however, should not be great at all.
C. Insulation: for an 8 x 10 you will need approximately 250 sq. ft. of foil-backed insulation @ $13.00 per 50 sq. ft. This comes to approximately $65.00.
Other materials, such as the polyethylene and cardboard can often be scavenged.
D. Nails, clamps, hinges, etc.
E. Hollow core door: 1¾ x 36 x 80 costs $20.00.

Note: The materials listed above are, of course, not complete, nor are the prices fixed. Lumber costs vary from area to area, as do the other materials. These are only approximations for the Los Angeles area. You might, however, want to consider scavenging as much of your lumber and other materials as possible. Talk to building contractors or construction workers and see if there isn't some way of buying your lumber as "seconds" off their sites. The best method of arriving at a practical price list is to figure the needs of your sauna yourself, the grade of wood you prefer to use, the type of foundation, etc., and go to your lumberyard. The salesman there will calculate for you an estimate on the spot for your needs. If that figure is too high for your budget, then start asking around and do some bargaining. A talented scavenger can cut the prices listed above by more than half.

bibliography

Johnson, Tom, and Miller, Tim. *The Sauna Book.* New York: Harper and Row, 1977.

Viherjuuri, H.J. *Sauna, The Finnish Bath.* Brattleboro, Vermont: Stephen Greene Press, 1972.

The Export Committee of the Finnish Sauna Society. *Finnish Sauna Culture.* Vaskiniemi, Helsinki 20 Finland.

The Finnish Sauna Society. *Let's Have a Sauna.* Helsinki.

index